The Kimsara Detective Agency

Bully Pulpit

Marty Meyer-Gad

Growth Affirm Press

published by
Growth Affirm Press

Copyright © 2016 by Marty Meyer-Gad
All rights reserved. Copyright under Berne Copyright Convention, Universal Copyright Convention, and Pan-American Copyright Convention. No part of this book may be reproduced, stored in a retrieval system, or transmitted in any form, or by any means, electronic, mechanical, photocopying, recording or otherwise, without prior permission of the author.

Thanks to my husband, Bruno for his support;
to Jo Schultz for suggestions and proof reading.
Thanks to the sixth, seventh and eight grade students I taught or met through extra curricular activities. Your curiosity inspired many of the characters in this series.

The Kimsara Detective Agency series:

        1. Dog Gone It
        2. Bully Pulpit

Growth Affirming Company
P.O. Box 3582
Mankato, MN 66002

www.growthaffirm.com

The Kimsara Detective Agency: Bully Pulpit
Title ID 6519236
ISBN 978-0001380442

The Kimsara Detective Agency

Bully Pulpit

Seventh grader, Sara Cowley gazed through the doors of Whistlestop Junior High School. The world outside sparkled as the January sun mocked the below freezing temperatures. Her best friend and classmate, Kim Porter, joined her, reporting, "Everyone's gathered at the usual table to celebrate."

"What a way to begin a new semester," beamed Sara. "That three day weekend with such nice temperatures has everyone in an upbeat mood."

"Since it's too cold to be outside we might as well return to school. With tests over and report cards not due until tomorrow, life is good," Kim added.

The Whistlestop Mexican Restaurant van pulled up. Sara and Kim held the school doors open as Paul Garcia and his father entered laden with two insulated carrying cases. After greetings they entered the cafeteria. A dozen members of the Kimsara Detective Agency gathered at their usual table waiting for a celebratory lunch. On the previous Friday they had been honored for stopping a dog-stealing operation.

Several were studying their group picture from various newspapers.

"Mr. Garcia, thanks for lunch," Sara said. Others echoed their appreciation as Paul and his father began spreading out the lunch.

"It's the least I can do for the Kimsara Detective Agency that gets our son, Diego, in the newspaper." Before anyone could question what they heard, he explained the various dishes as he unwrapped them. "You kids enjoy lunch. I have to get back to work." He tussled his blushing son's hair. A stream of "Thanks," followed him out.

"Diego?" questioned Kim looking at Paul.

"Paul is my first name but at home and in the restaurant everyone calls me by my middle name, 'Diego.'"

His best friend, Abdi, prompted, "Then why didn't your folks name you, 'Diego?'" He knew of the dual names. Being a Somali immigrant he wanted to know so much and often asked questions others found impolite. The slight blush of insecurity on his dark chocolate face went unnoticed.

After swallowing what he had been chewing, Paul answered, "I was named after my dad's buddy who fought with him in Afghanistan. He died. My dad said he had saved his life and so named me to honor him. My grandparents were upset at my name saying my dad was denying his Mexican heritage. So at home and the restaurant everyone uses my middle name."

"Should we call you, 'Diego?'" Conner proposed as he reached for another enchilada.

"You do and I'll slash the tires of your wheelchair," Paul threatened while glaring at Conner, surprising everyone with his uncharacteristic intimidation. "Seriously," he continued with a smile, "I like 'Paul' at school at least for now."

"Than 'Paul' it is and my wheels remain round," quipped Conner.

"Should we consider this the last meal for the Kimsara Detective Agency?" RT proposed. As one of the few eighth graders on the team he looked like a leader in his funereal black pants and button down shirt. He handled the intellectual technology (IT) for the group.

"No!" Sara declared with several echoing her. "Let's keep our eyes open. We are..."

Kim finished, "Kids In Modern Schools: Aware, Responsible, Active."

"Right, we should continue doing the Kimsara thing: Keeping Informed, Making Social Alliances, Reporting Anomalies," Abdi offered quoting himself from the award presentation ceremony. "Another case is bound to come up."

The Kimsara Detective Agency included a unique mix of seventh and eight graders who were constantly adding more to their number. For Sara Cowley the group allowed her a new identity. No one considered Sara as the girl who transferred because a car accident killed her parents and brother. She and her friends accepted Aunt Patty Cowley and Uncle Art Chaffins as her parents. Their neighbor, Kim, cemented their friendship early on by proposing they form the Kimsara Detective Agency, which quickly grew beyond the two of them.

Chapter 2

The next day began in a January grey haze, a prelude to the blizzard expected that evening. In case it arrived prematurely requiring early dismissal, report cards were passed out during first period homeroom.

Sara expected a C in Math and A's and B's in her other subjects. When she saw an A in Math her hand shot up to report, "There's a mistake on my report card."

Her homeroom teacher, Ms. Becky Watson, checked, "Are you sure, Sara?"

"No way is an A in Math right," Sara stated.

The room buzzed with similar objections to grades. Throughout the morning each period began with students wanting their grades checked. Teachers were baffled at some of the incorrect grades which didn't match the grades on their computer files.

At lunch everyone discussed grades. Kim claimed, "My grades are correct. Sara, why would you question a grade being too high?"

Sara explained, "I really didn't get Math when the school year started. It seemed so different from what I was used to. I was lucky to get a C on my assignments when the semester started. As I caught on, my grades have been rising, but there's no way they would average out to an A.

Abdi joined the group at the table questioning, "Are your grades right?" When most admitted they weren't. He acknowledged, "Mine definitely are not! I got a C in math. I've never gotten anything lower than an A- on my work and none of my assignments are missing. Mr. Carver is checking into it. The grade surprised him too."

"Maybe I got your A," Sara confessed.

Abdi continued, "Could the grades have just gotten mixed up? I got an A in phy ed. Me! I always get a C, which I deserve. I hate gym."

RT said, "I think someone hacked into the school's computer system."

Just then Vice-Principal Dickens walked by as students swamped him with questions about their grades. The teachers had already told him that the grades weren't right.

RT asked the vice principle, "Does the school have an IT person who could figure out who hacked into the system?"

"I don't think anyone hacked anything," the vice principal seethed.

"Have you changed grading programs?" considered Kim.

"No, it's the same one we've been using for three years," he acknowledged. "We don't have money in the budget to hire a computer geek to fix this mess."

"Vice Principal Dickens, I think I know someone who will do it for free. Her daughter is in first grade. She helps us in the Kimsara Detective Agency. Do you want me to check with her?" RT suggested.

The vice principal stood, raising his eyes and breathing in deeply searching for patience. How dare these impudent students think they could help.

RT quickly texted Officer Lee Petersen receiving an immediate text back. "She can stop by school around three-thirty today. Is that okay?"

He wanted to say it wasn't. He didn't want to face this mess let alone be accountable for it to an outsider. Yet, he had to face it.

"Yes," muttered the vice principal, "but what is this guru's name?"

"Oh, sorry. She's Officer Lee Petersen, the head of IT at the county sheriff's office. I think she would be trustworthy."

"If she's not, our county is in trouble," quipped Sara as she left the table with the rest, to return to classes.

Chapter 3

Vice Principal Dickens returned to his office, to make an announcement. "Please disregard the report card marks you have. Computer errors mixed up some grades. Once the system is fixed new report cards will be issued."

RT busily texted Officer Lee to see if she needed any additional information.

She answered immediately urging them to get as many grades which they knew were wrong.

RT texted the Kimsara network. "Round up every report card that has an obvious error and write what the correct grade should be. If you see report cards in the recycling bins pick them up. See if you can find the student and identify the wrong grades. Drop all your evidence in the chess pigeonhole in the office before you leave. Thanks."

Sara met RT in the hall later asking him, "Why do you want all the report cards in the chess pigeonhole?"

"Because the chess team disbanded so it's empty. It's also in the first row right as you go in the office."

"That makes sense. Do you need some help?"

"Officer Lee's is coming by at 3:30 today. Until she comes, we won't know. I plan on staying. I walk home and my folks get home after five so I won't be missed."

"My mom has to mail out an article today. Usually she doesn't get to town until 4 PM. The post office closes at 4:30. So if she follows her usual pattern, I can join you," Sara said while contacting her mom.

Her mother answered on the first ring. "Mom, could I stay late after school and catch a ride with you when you go to the post office?

"I can live with that. Thanks, Mom.

"I can stay but she's working out and doing some shopping too. She might not come before 6 PM."

"Good, see you in the school office later."

"Will do." On her way to her science class she passed her best friend, Kim, and conveyed the plan. She explained that if she stayed they could ride home together but it might not be until 6 PM.

"Sorry, I've got to get home right after school." Kim knew she couldn't stay because she promised to help her sister, Marcia, on a project after school. Kim sometimes envied Sara for being an only child until she realized she would miss Marcia and her brothers. Also she didn't like the idea of losing her parents.

Chapter 4

After school Sara entered the principal's office as RT and Abdi sorted the report cards they pulled from the chess pigeonhole.

RT explained, "This pile has grades obviously higher than they should be. That pile has grades lower than they should be. Any that we have no idea about are face down on the counter. Vice Principal Dickens is meeting with the teachers to see if they see blatant errors in the grades."

Just then the vice principal entered the room with a pile of computer printouts. "I gave each teacher a print out of students' grades. They highlighted any student who has grades much higher than they should be. The names with check marks in front of them are students whose grades are too low." He left promising to return.

RT, looking at his watch commented, "Officer Lee should be here any moment."

As if on cue, Officer Lee and her daughter, Scout, appeared at the door. She wheeled herself across the room to settle Scout in a corner, giving her a juice box and her traveling toy box. After greeting everyone Lee asked, "Have any of you been on the internet today?"

No one had.

Vice Principal Dickens returned, registered surprise and quickly hid it. "You must be Officer Lee Petersen from the sheriff's office," he noted while shaking her hand.

"Guilty as charged," she admitted. "Is there a computer here that can get on the internet?"

"Most of them can. That one over there on the secretary's desk is probably the most convenient one."

Officer Lee booted up the computer. The vice principal entered the proper password. The students were curious. She typed in "Whistlestop Junior High grades." On YouTube they watched report card grades changing before their eyes.

"We are working with YouTube to get the site shut down. Another site has already been shut down. It advertised that for a price you could have your grade or that of a friend or foe changed."

"Do you know who is running the site?" the vice principal asked.

"We don't. We do know that the changes were made from a computer in this school."

"That can't be," protested the vice principal. "We have a security system. The students can't get on the internet without a password. Only the teachers have passwords that let them on the internet. The students have a little access to a limited number of sites. Definitely not to the grade sites."

"Shut down the computer, Mr. Dickens," Officer Lee ordered.

He did as told.

Then she brought the computer up and without requesting the vice principal's password, went back to the internet. She brought up the grade files to everyone's astonishment. With a few strokes she added a new student, Nemo Wise, and began entering grades.

A red-faced vice principal wanted to know, "Where did you get my password?"

"From you!"

"How?"

"I watched you type in 1 2 3 4 5 6. Anyone watching can figure out your simple password anytime you log in."

Vice Principal Dickens was visibly upset. He had pinned his job security on his superior technology and security skills.

Chapter 5

"Who on the staff is responsible for internet security?" Officer Lee asked expecting the answer to be everyone.

"Maybe we shouldn't discuss security in front of the students," he admonished, dodging the question. Sara returned to the piles of papers by the pigeonholes with everyone else following her.

Officer Lee looked at him as he turned deeper shades of red. She had never liked this man who served as the vice principal to all the different divisions of the school. Suddenly she understood and requested he clarify his position. "You're the one responsible for technology in the whole Whistlestop school system, right?"

"Yes," he mumbled.

"Good," she said confusing him. "Most of the computers with internet access are in the media center, right?"

He nodded.

"How late is the media center open?"

"We have volunteer parents staffing it most nights from after school until 8 PM," he said.

"Do you have a list of all the computer serial numbers?"

"Yes, I'll get it," he offered, relieved to leave the room. The students looked intensely interested in the papers they shuffled.

Officer Lee wheeled over to them and asked, "Were you able to acquire some of the report cards with obvious changes?"

"Yes, these have grades that went up significantly," pointed out RT.

"These went down." added Sara, pointing to another pile.

Abdi further explained, "But these printouts are better because they were marked by the teachers who looked over the grades. Six students had all their grades changed to straight As."

"Good work, Abdi," complimented Officer Lee.

As everyone looked over the list, Sara made a diagram. Jack Becker, Tyler Freeman and maybe James Arnt could be the ring leaders. Bennu Bashara, Herman Montel, and Tony Criscitelli wouldn't have the computer smarts but they would have the money to pay to have it done.

"Why were some of my grades changed?" pressed Sara.

Officer Lee answered, "Are any of these guys your boyfriend?"

"Please," glowered Sara rolling her eyes in disbelief, "I don't have time for that. I'll wait until high school."

"Have any of these boys tried to be your boyfriend?"

Sara admitted, "Tony has asked me out a couple of times but I always refused him."

Officer Lee proposed, "Could he be trying to win your favor by doing favors for you?"

"I never thought about it like that. It's a waste of his time and money. All he ever talks about is being rich enough to do whatever he likes."

"How is he with computers?" Officer Lee wondered.

"I don't think very good. He always pays Jack or Tyler to help him on the computer," said Abdi.

Chapter 6

The vice principal returned, announcing, "Here's the list of computer serial numbers."

"Thanks," then upon examining the paper Officer Lee noted, "But this just tells you what computers you have. It doesn't tell you where the computers are."

"Of course not," he said indignantly. "When we do deep cleaning in the summer, computers get moved around. It doesn't make sense to keep a list since the computer placement isn't stable."

She pulled out a paper with an email address on it instructing them to: "Please go to every computer. Log on and send an email identifying what room you're in to this address. Also, include the serial number of the computer." She showed them where to find it.

The vice principal feeling left out muttered, "The students can't email without a teacher's password."

"If you need a password, try the following passwords." She handed each a sheet of the most common passwords. "Ideally I would like to see you working in teams of two, but with only three..."

The office door opened and a boy dressed in blue sweats entered. "Hi, everyone. Sorry I'm late. I left practice as soon as I could."

Abdi greeted him. "Paul, glad you could make it. I invited Paul to join us. Hope that's okay, though we should probably be in different groups."

Paul continued, "Because we think alike."

"Okay, Paul and I will take the east wing," RT suggested.

Sara added, "Then Abdi and I will do the west wing."

"If you can't email from the computer, just write down its serial number and location," Officer Lee advised.

The students were able to email from every computer in the school. For some they used "Password." For most, they found the password written somewhere on the computer. They also found a second password which got them to Nemo's report card. When they were able to do so both groups, thanks to the synchronicity of Paul and Abdi, left the following message: *Grade change possible* followed by the room and computer number.

They converged at the media center with its computer lab. There no passwords were visible. By using the teachers passwords they had learned, they easily emailed from each computer. By then the comment section of Nemo's grades was full. So they created another student Shemo Wise and continued documenting that they could get to this grading file from any computer in the school.

In thirty minutes the students returned to the school office.

Chapter 7

Officer Lee asked, "How did it go? Any computers you couldn't access?"

"None," RT replied as Officer Lee scrolled through 96 emails, one from each computer in the school. She brought up Nemo's report card file with 50 comments. She then found Shemo's file with 46 comments.

Officer Lee checked, "How many computers does the school have?"

"One hundred," the vice principal declared.

"So you have four computers in the offices here?" questioned Abdi.

Having a seventh grader question him as he faced a compromising situation, made him rethink his answer. "Actually we have 103 computers. Five are in the offices, but two of them are older models that can't connect to the internet. So we have three that can access the grade files in the office."

Officer Lee had been checking the grading software. She asked, "Where is the computer with the serial number mm1394085? It's not on the list of checked computers, but it has made many grade entries."

"Then it's not in this building," emphatically barked the vice principal.

"It has to be. It's coming through your internal network," she maintained.

"Can't be," he argued.

After a few minutes of awkward silence, Paul realized, "The computer from the gym isn't on the list. We didn't check it out."

Abdi echoed, "Neither did we."

"So what about the computer in the coaches' office, Mr. Dickens?" needled RT.

"I forgot about that one," a sheepish vice principal confessed.

"We'll email you from it," promised Abdi as he and Paul headed out.

Within minutes an email came through stating, "*Easiest one yet. The 'locked' gym door opened easily and all the passwords are in plain sight. The serial number on the computer is mm1394085.*"

"Who are your coaches?" demanded Officer Lee.

"Coach Becker teaches all the gym classes and a variety of teachers coach the various sports. Coach Becker only does football."

Sara observed, "Isn't Coach Becker Jack's father?"

"Yes," admitted the vice principal.

Paul added, "Jack doesn't participate in any sports but he's always in the coaching office."

The vice principal explained, "He does his homework there while waiting for his father for a ride home."

Changing the subject Officer Lee questioned, "How often do you backup the files?"

He said, "Once a week."

"Who does the back up?" asked Officer Lee.

In harmony the students cried, "Mrs. Freeman, Tyler's mom."

"Where are the backup files kept?" she inquired.

A blushing vice principal conceded, "I don't know."

"They're in the media center," RT claimed. "I'll go get them." He went to the media center and brought back a box of discs. "These are the media center's backup files."

The vice principal challenged, "How did you know about the backups, Mr. Tracy?"

"I have been backing up files for the past two years."

"Why?" the vice principal entreated.

"Vice Principal Dickens, I was alone in the media center one day when Mrs. Freeman asked if I knew how to back up files. I told her I did. Then she asked me to back up the grade file. She left. She came back in a weird state and asked if I would do it every week. When I asked her how many weeks I should keep, she said one was fine and I should use the same disc every week."

"Did you?" urged Abdi.

"No, there are four discs in the box. The first disc has the last backup. I didn't think one week was enough. So I rotated them so there are four weeks of files." He turned over the box to reveal a small calendar taped to the bottom of the disc box. "I write the letter of the disc on the calendar so I can keep track of what disc to use next."

"Mr. Dickens, I need to head home. May I take all the discs, except the current one, home with me?" asked Officer Lee.

He wanted to give his usual speech that school security made the removal impossible. Then realizing security didn't exist in his school, he agreed.

Officer Lee took her briefcase from the side of her wheel chair and deposited the discs. She also took the printouts and the pile of report cards with grades that were too high or too low. She admitted, "Mr. Dickens I cannot guarantee I'll get this information back to you in the morning but I'll get it back to you as soon as I can." She wheeled over to her daughter and helped her pack up her toys before leaving.

Chapter 8

The next day the Kimsara regulars gathered at lunch. RT described how they had checked all the computers.

Conner interrupted, "Are you saying the grades had been hacked from a school computer?"

"Officer Lee thinks so," acknowledged Sara.

"Do you know which one was used?" asked Emma.

Sara not wanting to give incorrect information quickly replied, "We might have the right one. Officer Lee is double checking before any announcement is made. She took the printouts and backup discs to examine."

"That explains why they announced grades may be delayed a week," commented Emma.

"My brother found a YouTube video showing the grades being changed. When I tried to find it, I couldn't," Kim announced.

"The police were aware of it. Looks like they succeeded in getting it removed," reported RT.

"Sara, you were right. There is more the Kimsara Detective Agency can do," Paul admitted.

"While Officer Lee checks on the computer files, I'd like us to solve another mystery," proposed Abdi.

"What mystery?" several asked.

Abdi stood to make his point. "Does anyone know what happened to Andy Parta?"

"The last day we saw him at school was the day he..." Paul searched for words.

"Accused God of causing the typhoon in the Philippines," recalled Sara.

"I saw him leave school with his dad that day," reported Emma. "He hasn't been seen since."

"Did his dad look mad enough to kill him?" Paul cautiously suggested.

"No, more sad than mad," remembered Emily.

"The rumors that Andy's dad killed him are wrong. My dad talked to Andy's dad that day. He transferred him to another school," Sara explained. "Until Andy comes back to school, I think he'll remain a mystery,"

As the group scattered from lunch each one wondered about Andy and his whereabouts. Sara felt guilty and responsible for his plight. She had yelled at him for saying that God sent the typhoon because the people were sinning. She also called him out for saying her parents were in hell for not going to church every Sunday. She knew he was wrong.

Anytime she felt guilty she remembered his smug face as he passed her on his way to the principal's office. Her guilt subsided.

Chapter 9

Andy Parta had been comfortable frequenting the principal's office. He had expected persecution for his Christian beliefs. On that fateful day several months ago he thought he knew exactly what the principal would say. She surprised him by telling him to have a seat outside her office by the secretary's desk. She closed the door and called Andy's father. Months ago he had confided his worries over his son's religious zeal and was researching possible programs to help him. In accord with his previous request she explained what had happened. He seemed to comprehend its severity. His wife's fundamentalism helped turn their son into a righteous snob. Her righteousness didn't allow her to accept the divorce he requested.

Being a lawyer and having discussed the issue with colleagues he began putting "reality therapy" to work. He called his wife and told her to meet him at 2 PM at the courthouse. He also told her Andy had some trouble at school but talking about it could wait until they saw each other.

The principal called Andy into her inner office. When he shuffled in she began, "Andy, tell me what happened."

"People don't believe that God doesn't like sinners and kills them."

"That's what you believe, right? Does everyone have to believe what you believe?"

"Well, Abdi doesn't because he's Muslim."

"Do you know what he believes?"

"He believes in Allah and not in Jesus Christ, so he can't be saved."

"According to you he can't. Andy, this is not a religious school." Andy rolled his eyes at the familiar words. "This is a country where government and religion are separate. You cannot impose your religious views on anyone while you are in school."

"Mom wants me to go to a Christian school where the truth is taught."

"But she hasn't put you in one. You are here in public school. Go eat your lunch. When the class bell rings return to this office."

"Yes, Principal Jones," he declared with his insolent head held high. He knew his mother would be so proud of him standing up for the truth. Every Christian has to suffer because the world does not understand them.

After lunch Andy, began settling his self-righteous self in homeroom, when he was again called to the principal's office. She handed him some paper and a pen, then thought better of it. Instead she handed him a laptop dedicated to writing, giving him no temptation to play games or go on line. "I want you to document what you said and why you said it."

"Yes, Principal Jones." He wondered if he heard right. "You want me to write what happened and why I did what I did."

"Yes, there's a desk by the secretary's you can use. Let her know when you're finished."

"Okay." Andy felt so good about being able to tell the whole story. Maybe he would redeem Principal Jones by what he wrote.

Constant interruptions from spellcheck slowed Andy's progress. After a quick review of what happened, he luxuriated in preaching the truth. Words flowed quickly. When he finished he told the secretary. She handed him a paper with the instructions: "Pretend you are Sara and write how she feels about what you said to her."

"I don't get it."

The secretary explained, "You are putting yourself in Sara's shoes. You may have to think about it. Imagine what she thought and how she felt."

During the conversation, the secretary had printed out Andy's writings and also emailed them to the principal. She disengaged the Wifi and returned the laptop to him opened to a new file.

For a half hour Andy thought, dribbling a word here and there on the screen. He felt sorry for the unsaved girl.

Finally a few sentences came together. He approached the secretary. "That was hard. Is this okay?"

"For now it is. I'll open a new file for you to write an apology to Sara."

"Why, I didn't do anything wrong?"

"You hurt her feelings. You didn't respect her and what she has experienced. You probably hurt her more than if you had given her a black eye. Would you understand how to apologize to someone you punched?"

"I don't punch people. I'm the one getting punched."

"Okay what kind of an apology would you want from someone who beat you up. That's the kind of apology you owe Sara for hurting her."

Andy slunk back to the desk thinking. His apology highlighted him being sorry that she was wrong. The only thing he held himself responsible for was being a Christian. He noted he knew he wasn't allowed to say, "God," in school. He also acknowledged Christians were supposed to suffer.

Sara never saw that apology.

Chapter 10

All of his writing for that day was emailed to his father, Joseph Parta, as he had requested. When Mr. Parta picked Andy up after school Andy noticed a suitcase in the backseat. His father felt his son's radical religious beliefs were dangerous. He would not let him become the Christian equivalent of a terrorist. On the other hand his wife fully supported their son's radicalism. For months he had researched ways Andy could develop a more social conscience. Andy's actions that day convinced him the time to act had arrived.

As he fastened his seatbelt Andy asked, "You going somewhere, Dad?"

"No, you are, Son."

"What?"

"Did you write this?" he demanded handing him printouts of that day's writing.

While Andy made a cursory examination, his dad asked, "May I see your phone and wallet?"

While mindlessly passing his phone and wallet to his father, Andy admitted, "Yes, Father. Why?"

"Son, you are dead sure you have the truth about religion. Well, you don't. I have tried over and over to get that through your head."

"But Mom says..."

"Your mother is encouraging you on a very destructive path. Look at the bottom papers. Based on the writings you have in your hand, I got a restraining order against your mother. She cannot have any contact with you."

"Come on, Dad, we live in the same house."

"Not anymore." He paused for effect. Andy looked confused. "You are going to live with a Quaker community that has agreed to act as your boarding school. You may not call or write your mother until the court order is lifted."

Andy was stunned. He couldn't wrap his head around the words. He felt scared, angry, confused. He wanted to scream, to kill his hell-bound father.

They exited Minnesota and began traveling through Wisconsin. No words were spoken during their dinner stop. Joseph ordered his son's favorites. Andy's hunger overrode his decision to refuse to eat. He inhaled the meal. His habit of gratitude refused to be silenced. Surprising himself, he thanked his father for dinner. They returned to the car and silence.

Finally after the sun had set they stopped in front of a big house. "We're here," his father announced while removing Andy's suitcase. He opened the passenger car door, removed the seatbelt and pulled his son to his feet.

"Son, do I have to carry you or pull you by your hand?" he threatened. Without waiting for an answer he turned and walked toward the house. Andy stumbled behind, quickening his step as his father opened the door. Once inside the door his father introduced him to a few people who welcomed him.

The one named, Quinn, took his suitcase. Andy refused to make eye contact with his father who apologized. "Son, you need help. I'm sorry I couldn't find an easier way to help you. I've known Quinn all my life and so feel comfortable trusting him with your life. Listen to him. If you want to get in touch with me, let Quinn know and he'll arrange it."

"But my backpack and phone!"

Quinn tried calming him, "You won't need them." He set down the suitcase, shook hands with Andy's father. Andy clenched his arms in front of him refusing any contact with his father, who turned and walked to the car. Tears streamed down the faces of both. Joseph hoped he was doing the right thing.

Chapter 11

Once Quinn showed him the room they would share, Andy knew it was real. Shock grew when he opened his suitcase and found only underwear, pajamas and a garbage bag filled with his legos. His drawers were filled with clothes, clothes that weren't his style and looked like someone had already worn them.

Andy's anger grew after his father dropped him off. His stubborn, defiant stand weakened as Quinn patiently waited for him to do what he was told. Andy wished he would yell at him so he could yell back. But Quinn wouldn't get pulled into his game. So Andy did as he was told.

The next morning after eating oatmeal for the first time in his life, Quinn approached Andy. "Ready for school, Son."

Andy's anger flared at being called "Son," but looking around him and not seeing any allies, he calmly rose to his feet, carried his dishes to the proper window and followed Quinn. They rode in silence to a dilapidated school. Andy's heart sank as Quinn parked, saying, "Welcome to your new school." He then handed him a ratty looking backpack containing his necessary supplies.

Andy, embarrassed by the ragged backpack anchored it to his back was relieved he couldn't see it. They walked into the principal's office. Quinn introduced Andy saying his school records should arrive in a day or two.

The principal corrected him. "His father dropped them off this morning."

Andy's eyes widened. This was no joke. Would he be in this school for the rest of the year, the rest of his life? His heart sank. Tears formed. He tried to keep them in. When Quinn handed him a tissue, he sheepishly dabbed them away. He shuffled behind them.

"Here's your classroom, Andy." The principal held out an un-shook hand. A nudge from Quinn did not change the situation so both men ignored it.

"Welcome aboard," the principal declared before walking into the room to introduce Andy to his teacher who met them at the doorway To Andy's astonishment Quinn walked into the room. He sat down next to a student. They began working together.

Andy stood in the doorway wishing he could run away, knowing he had no place to go. Starting with the student working with Quinn, each began introducing themselves.

Andy looked around at his classmates. They were definitely poorer than him. The clothes he was embarrassed to wear that morning fit right in. He had planned on wearing his clothes from yesterday, but couldn't find them.

As each child sat down he mentally labelled each a "Loser."

A student named Nikita stood up revealing, "I came here from Russia with my mother. My father is an astronaut and will live with us when he retires. Welcome to our class, Andy."

"Liar," Andy erroneously thought.

A slip of a girl did not stand up but raised her hand from her wheelchair, toggling it into a better position to see Andy. "I'm Shelley. I'm in a wheelchair because when I was young I tried to fly off our house roof."

Andy turned red as a chuckle escaped him. He apologized, "I'm sorry."

"Ah that's okay. I try to make people laugh when I tell them my story. I was such a dumb kid to try it. I messed up my body. I do physical therapy to help heal my legs. My goal is to walk down the aisle at my high school graduation."

"Nice to meet you, Shelley. I hope you reach your goal."

"Thank you." she said as she toggled her chair back behind her desk.

When everyone finished the teacher in a very serious tone, instructed, "Now, Andy, will you please name everyone of your 37 classmates? Come to the front to do it."

In horror he walked to the front staring into the teacher's eyes of steel. He relaxed when he turned around. Each child held up a name tag. He half expected to hear the teacher say, "Gotcha." He went down the rows reading each name. With only twenty in a classroom in his former school, he knew change awaited him.

Chapter 12

Andy was ahead in most subjects, making classes effortless. Just when he began feeling bored breezing along, his teacher requested, "Will you please help Sam Michel with his math? Don't do it for him. Just explain how it is done and watch him do it."

Andy took his chair and put it next to Sam's desk. Sam smelled and Andy's face registered the fact. Sam quietly admitted, "Sorry, I smell. We don't have a house right now. So we sleep in our car. We usually wash up at McDonald's or Walmart but Mom didn't have enough gas to take me there. Maybe tonight."

His words disorientated Andy who opened Sam's book to the right page. He asked him to explain the example in the book. Getting no response he continued, "It shows the fraction one half equals the fraction two fourths because you multiply the denominator and the numerator by two." Seeing Sam's face go blank he rephrased it again and again until Sam started to understand.

Hoping the idea of a common denominator finally registered, he had Sam do one by himself. He glowed when told it was right. He needed help on the next one but continued to get more right."

Andy's mind wandered a bit. Fractions, fractions in seventh grade. Didn't we do them in fourth grade? The teacher had started the class with examples of using fractions in equations. When they moved on to another subject, Andy noticed that in fact Sam had a fourth grade math book.

Lunch was strange. No computer needed your lunch number. No one reminded kids their lunch accounts were getting low. Andy looked for the missing salad bar and entrée choices. Instead everyone got the same hot dish of beans and rice with some specs of meat in it, peas and an apple. The bread offered wasn't pure white like the bread he ate at home, so he passed it up.

Everyone ate with very little talking. Some put their bread and apple in their pockets. He planned to leave the peas on his plate until he saw every plate around him totally cleaned. He ate the peas.

On the way home Andy asked Quinn, "Why did you stay in my classroom all day?"

"I'm a teacher's aid, helping students who are behind."

"Why weren't you helping Sam. He's really behind."

"Yes, he is. I helped him yesterday. Today you were helping him."

"Sam is homeless."

"I know."

"Why doesn't Sam come and live with the Quakers?"

"It's not that simple, Andy. People without homes need to want help. Often there is a reason why they lost their home.

They have to take care of that before they are ready for a home."

"Really?"

After a few miles of silence, Andy changed the subject. "Why don't they serve white bread at school?"

"For the same reason we don't serve it at home, because it is not good for you. The whole grain breads they serve are a lot healthier. Didn't you try the bread?"

"No, I had enough with the hot dish. Why didn't I have to pay for lunch?"

"Because your father already paid for your lunches for the whole year."

"Whole year," boomeranged through Andy's mind not allowing him to comprehend Quinn's explanation.

"The few who can afford to pay for their lunches pay in the office once a week or once a month. If their parents lose their job or have an unexpected bill, the students still get lunch."

Andy had a lot to think over for the rest of the ride as "whole year" rumbled from his head to his stomach.

Chapter 13

Andy slowly began making friends. From the first day he wanted an easy explanation for transferring to that school. Should he say that his dad got mad at him and made him transfer? Should he admit he tried to convert people and his father wanted him to stop but feared he wouldn't change? Should he say he's waiting for his mother to rescue him? He constantly wondered why she hadn't. His new friends never asked why.

Others, the only ones with cell phones, were big and loud and forever taunting other students. One day, his turn came. He walked out to the playground when three boys stepped in front of him.

"Hey, misfit what school threw you out?"

He tried to walk away when the biggest of them, the one with "Denny" embroidered on his jacket, walked into him. Andy kept on backing up until flat against the playground fence. Denny growled in his face, "Norman, Butch and I own the playground. There's only one rule. You got to pay to use it. How much money do you have on you, Geek?"

"Nothing," Andy muttered sadly realizing for the first time in his life he didn't have any money.

"Come on you freak, everyone has some money on him. Turn out those pockets."

Andy did as told. Only an eraser fell out.

The bell rang to resume classes. Butch grabbed Andy's shirt, threatening, "You better have $5 for us tomorrow, or else."

The "or else" ricocheted in his head until his stomach hurt.

When he entered the classroom, Quinn approached him. "You, okay?"

"I don't know," he admitted with confusion.

"Are you sick?"

"Sort of, but it's not the kind of sickness that going home will help. Can we talk more about this after school?"

"Sure can."

Andy spent the rest of the day in turmoil. If he told Quinn what had happened would he mock him for not being able to stand up for himself? Or, would Quinn make him go and report what happened to the principal, getting him into even more hot water with the trio?

How could he get five dollars for tomorrow? He always had at least five dollars in his wallet. But his father had his wallet. He moved in a daze while transitioning from subject to subject. The final school bell rang too soon. Instead of getting ready to go home, Andy just sat bemoaning his crumbled world.

Quinn came up from behind and tousled his hair. "Are you planning on sleeping at school tonight?"

"No," Andy muttered and then with robot like movements he gathered his things into his tattered backpack and followed Quinn to the car.

"Rough day?" Quinn commented as he pulled on to the highway.

Andy just sighed.

"What happened on the playground today?"

"Nothing."

"It didn't look like nothing to me. You were with a pretty dangerous bunch. Did they threaten you?"

"Kind of." Andy wanted the conversation to end. He did not want to be a snitch but he also didn't want to be picked on. He took some consolation knowing the three thugs were hell bound.

"Okay, start at the beginning and tell me what happened."

Andy didn't want to but at the same time he couldn't keep it in. He thought of what he had done back home. The realization hit him: "I'm a bully."

"Where did that come from?"

"Those three guys demanded I pay them money to be on the playground. As you know, I don't have any money. They checked all my pockets. When they couldn't find any money they told me I had to bring them $5 tomorrow, or else?"

"Or else, what?"

"I don't know and I don't think I want to know. What should I do, Quinn?"

"What do you want to do?"

"Go back home and back to my old school."

"Okay that's not a possibility. You know it. Do you want to give them the money?"

"No, because they'll keep demanding more."

"Are you sure?"

"That's what the kids at my old school did."

"Did they threaten you at your old school?"

"No, because I was one of them."

"Is that why you've changed schools and are living with us?"

"Possibly."

Chapter 14

"Andy, what student did you harass the most?"

"Abdi Ibraham," he immediately responded.

"Why did you pick on him?"

"Because he's a Muslim so he is going to hell if he doesn't become a Christian."

"A Christian, loving and kind, like you?" Quinn chided.

Andy's blush revealed a lot. He tried to defend himself. "Well, don't you have to believe in Jesus Christ to get to heaven?"

"I don't think so. Do you know who the Taliban are?"

"Terrorists."

"What do these terrorists want?"

"Control of the world?"

"How do they want to control the world?"

"By making everyone follow their rules. Women can't be seen and are considered less than men. Anyone who does not believe like they do, they want to kill," Andy spouted. Then he added, "Quinn, am I just like the Taliban?"

"Why would you say that?"

"Because I picked on everyone who I didn't think practiced religion right."

"Is that wrong?" When no answer came, Quinn added, "Think about it."

Andy thought about it for a full week. Finally one day on the way home Andy admitted, "It is wrong."

In surprise, Quinn countered, "Where did that come from? What are you talking about?"

"It's wrong to tell other people what they have to believe in. My classmates in Whistlestop must think I'm a real creep."

"What are you going to do about it?" Quinn pressed as they left the car.

"What can I do?" Andy sincerely wondered.

"Do you have much homework?"

"No, I finished it in school."

"Then may I suggest an activity for this evening?"

"I'm sure it's not to watch TV. Is there even a TV in the house?"

"Yes, but it's seldom on."

"So what are you suggesting for this evening?" Andy cautiously inquired.

"Remember you have dish duty tonight."

"Oh, I almost forgot. What do I have to do for dish duty?"

"Show up and do what people tell you to do."

"Will it take all night?

"No, usually under an hour giving you plenty of time for a project I would like to suggest."

"What's the project?"

"You've avoided the bullies all week by eating slow, volunteering for lunch time tasks and hiding in the bathroom. Is that what Abdi did when he saw you?"

"I don't think so. In a way he wasn't a coward like me. He just took it. He never argued, but I never threatened to beat him up. Come to think of it I never felt good after I criticized him like I did with some of the others. Still I'd look for him and say some really mean things, hoping I'd feel better."

"Did it work?"

"Never," Andy pouted.

"Tonight, write Abdi a letter, apologizing for what you did."

Andy excused himself from the unwanted task with, "But I don't have his address."

"I'll get that for you."

"Can...May I use the computer in the library to write the letter?"

"No, but you can take some of the copy paper from the library printer for your letter."

Andy didn't think he could feel sadder as he headed to the dining room. Allison stood by the cubbies where everyone put the cloth napkins they used for meals. Perched above the cubbies a doll balanced in a cardboard crib. When people passed the doll it would laugh. Pretty soon everyone, including Andy, chuckled.

The dinner of squash lasagna sounded horrible. Andy passed it by until he realized there wasn't anything else to eat. As he turned back, a man removing a healthy slice from the pan realized Andy's predicament. He smiled at him as he put the generous portion on Andy's plate. Andy thanked him even though he felt like gagging. He braced himself as he took the first bite, astonished that it tasted good.

Surprisingly he enjoyed doing dishes after dinner. Allison led the crew and kept parking her doll in different places so every time someone passed by it would laugh. The time passed quickly and soon Andy sat in the library with a pen, pencil and paper. He would write and rip it up and then repeat the routine.

Chapter 15

Andy accepted he had been a bully but couldn't wrap his head around being a terrorist. He couldn't be that evil. The foreign language of apologies didn't flow easily onto his paper. Finally he had:

Dear Abdi,

I am sorry for putting down your religion and saying you were going to hell. I didn't think that I was a bully but I felt comfortable being one. I thought I was a good bully. I didn't smash in kids faces or take their lunch money. I thought I was making sure people got to heaven. I've had a lot of time to think about what I did.

The day I made Sara cry, my dad pulled me out of school. He didn't take me home. I wasn't even able to say goodbye to my mom or pack my clothes.

He drove me to this Quaker place to live. He took away my wallet, phone and tablet.

I do not have a computer to use. That's why I am writing this and not typing it. It's strange to write with a pen and not do this on my computer.

Dad said he was taking me to a boarding school. I thought it was like a military academy but it's not. I live with the Quakers. I have a -- I don't know what to call him. His name is Quinn. We share a room. He drives me to school each day. It's a poor public school. I have no money which seems strange. I don't watch TV. At first I was very angry but I think I am becoming a better person.

The church my mom and I went to claimed it was the only way to get to heaven. We were supposed to bring as many people with us as possible by getting them to proclaim Jesus as their Lord and Savior. I now know that I or my church don't have control over who gets into heaven. A loving God does. I wonder if God finds our church services boring.

Wanting to get people to heaven is a good thing. Now I realize that wasn't my real reason. I told people they're going to hell because that made me better than them. I was going to heaven and they weren't. I am so sorry for judging you. I'm really sorry I was so mean.

You are the first person from school I have been able to contact.

Quinn said he'd put your address on the envelope. I don't even know my own address. I hope he puts it on the envelope. Then you can write me back and let me know if you forgive me.

I miss home and school. It makes me feel good to have some contact with my old life by being able to write to you.

I hope you are not being teased too much. I am sorry for what I did to you. Please forgive me.

Your friend,
Andy Parta

Chapter 16

Andy often missed his mother. He spoke frequently to his father. At first he begged his father to let him come home and hung up in anger when his father didn't agree. As he settled in, he shared school incidents. He always asked to speak to his mother. She was never home. He wondered where she was and whether the restraining order his dad mentioned had something to do with not being able to talk to her. He smothered thoughts of divorce anytime they surfaced.

The next evening he asked Quinn if he could write her a letter. Quinn's quick yes surprised him. Not only did he agree, he signed into the library computer so Andy could type the letter. Andy didn't know how to begin. Should he use Mom? Definitely not Mommy. He decided to begin his letter with:

Dear Mother,

    I miss you so much. Sorry I have not been able to talk to you on the phone. I call Dad often and hope he tells you that I am okay.

    This is hard for me to write because I don't want to say you are wrong. Maybe if I knew what was right this would be easier. But I don't know. I do know that I was a bully at school. I had no real friends. I went around telling people they were going to hell if they didn't believe like I did. That was wrong. Heaven is a big place and God can let in whoever God wants. I'm not God. Religion is supposed to make us better people. Mine was making me obnoxious.

    Andy was grateful he had spell check.

    I am well. I'm eating more vegetables than I ever knew existed. I miss your cooking.

    I was ahead in most of my classes when I started at my new school.

    He wondered if he should he be honest and say he was forced? That might upset his mother.

So I have been able to help some kids catch up. Now I am learning new things and with my new friends we are learning together.

When I came I didn't bring the nice clothes you bought me. In the drawers I found clean clothes that definitely had been worn before. I was too mad to be embarrassed about my clothes when I started at school here. But now I see, my clothes would have stuck out. No one in school wears new clothes. New clothes are saved for Sundays and holidays.

I never realized how good I had it. I took so much for granted.

Thanks, Mom, for everything you did for me. I wish I could see you or at least talk to you soon.

Love,
Andy

He printed the letter and gave it to Quinn before getting ready for bed. He smiled the next morning when he saw the envelope on the dash addressed to his mother. He did not know that a second letter joined his. It read:

Dear Mrs. Parta,

Andy's return address, a P.O. Box, is on the envelope if you should decide to write back to him. Be aware that I will be reading his letters before he gets them. Your husband, and I agree, thought Andy was heading down the road to becoming a Christian Taliban, if their is such a thing. He was too busy condemning his classmates to make friends. He followed the profile of too many school shooters.

Your husband is wise in his commitment to radically change Andy's course in life.

Any letters you send that put him back on the road to righteous superiority will not be given to your son. Please do write back giving him encouragement to become a normal, happy boy that not only fits in with his peers but enables him to be a positive influence in the world.

If you have any questions, do not hesitate to write to me or email me at Quinn71@ Quakers.com.

Wishing you the best,
Quinn Black

☙

On the way to school Quinn stopped so Andy could put the letter in the post office drop box.

Chapter 17

On Thursday, back in Whistlestop, Sara got a text from Officer Lee. *Could KDA meet her in the principal's office after school today?* Sara texted her mother getting her permission to stay late. She forwarded the message to everyone in their group.

After the dismissal bell rang Abdi, RT, Conner, Emma, Paul, Kim and Sara gathered outside the school office waiting for Officer Lee. The vice principal invited the group into the large conference room.

As soon as they settled, Officer Lee rolled in. After settling her daughter, she passed around around a paper. She explained, "Here is a chart of what days and times the changes were made. The last columns indicates which computer generated the changes. This has become a police investigation so no one in this room can tell anyone what is said here. That includes you, Vice Principal Dickens.

"Does the school have security cameras?" she asked.

"A few," the vice principal noted.

"Would you please pull the tapes from any camera near any of these listed computers on the days and times noted?"

"That will take awhile since Mrs. Freeman from the media center is out for a month or more recovering from surgery," he confessed. He had no idea where the information was stored.

Abdi declared, "I think I can get the shots you need."

"So can I," revealed RT. He pulled out the spare flash drive he always carried.

Officer Lee caught the surprised expression on the vice principal's face as the two left.

Moments later they returned with the flash drive containing the backup of the security cameras.

As the vice principal sputtered, "How..." his voice trailed off. He turned his back on the group, shuffling toward the door.

Everyone watched him retreat, looking at each other in bewilderment.

Then Officer Lee's phone rang. She wheeled away from the table to the opposite end of the room.

Sara shrugged her shoulders. The others shook their heads in disbelief.

Officer Lee returned with, "Sorry, a change of plans. I'll be back tomorrow at 8 AM with a detective. The district attorney is determined to try this case and wants to make sure there is no question about the chain of command.

"Sorry, I got you together for nothing." As she gathered her papers she repeated, "Remember anything you heard here can't be repeated."

"Not even to the rest of the detective agency?" tested Paul.

"Right, you can tell them that I thought I had a lead you could research but in the end it didn't work out. So they didn't miss anything. Does everyone understand that secrecy is vitally important?"

They all did.

Sara helped her gather Scout's things and pack them up. She put the traveling toy box in its place on the wheelchair.

Scout raised her hand to Sara. She took it. The three of them headed to the parking lot.

Chapter 18

The next day, Officer Lee returned with Detective Cory Watkins. Neither of them had police uniforms on so as far as the students knew they were computer consultants fixing the glitch that mixed up the grades. They took over the media center. All of the computers in question had cameras aimed at them.

By noon they had all the information they needed. A half hour before school ended, six students were called to the principal's office. Once there the police handcuffed them and arrested them for computer tampering, destruction of school property and theft of security codes. While the students were being processed the school secretary and principal called their parents letting them know that their children were being arrested and taken to the county jail.

The students were tucked into police cars and driven away from school before the final bell rang. They were advised not to say anything until they were questioned in the presence of their parents.

Jack Becker's father arrived at the police station first. He insisted, "You've blown things out of proportion. It was just an adolescent prank. No one got hurt by it. Get my son, so I can take him home and take care of the matter."

"Sir, it's not that easy. I can let you see your son but taking him home is premature," the officer on duty explained.

"Do I need to get a lawyer?"

"A good lawyer might help."

James Arnt's mother came with her brother, a lawyer. She apologized for what her son had done. Her brother arranged for her to see him.

Tyler Freeman presented a different story. His father was out of town. His mother, still not able to drive, recruited her brother to pick her up. He volunteered to bring along his wife, a lawyer.

Herman Montel's father told the police to let him rot in jail. He was too busy to be concerned about his son's childish prank. If the police didn't have any real crimes to pursue, must they invent charges against the teen population.

The big surprise in the group wore a hijab, a girl named Bennu Bashara, the ring leader. She covered her head like most of the Muslim girls in school. However her hijab and long dresses were always fine satin. When her mother answered the phone she could not fathom what was happening to her daughter. Her husband didn't answer his cell phone. In near panic, she called her Imam who agree to meet her at the police station.

District Attorney Faith Waters wanted to create an model case that would discourage computer fraud in all schools. Her desire for national attention faltered. These were minors. Nameless publicity wouldn't make the impact she wanted. Reluctantly she agreed to release them to their parents.

"School Computers Hacked," headlined the next day's newspaper. Since all were minors, no names appeared. None were needed. Everyone in school knew who had been called to the office. When each returned to school, their inability to meet the gaze of others confirmed it.

Eventually they had their day in juvenile court which sentenced them to parole with strict conditions: a year without internet access, mandatory community service and some serious fines.

After Herman Montel Senior saw a side of his son he had ignored he offered to lend the school five dedicated laptop computers. These would allow the students access to internal encyclopedias and receive school assignments and emails but not send any out. Every school day they reported to the office with a flash drive with their assignments which were downloaded, sent through the standard anti-plagiarizing software and then to their teachers' inboxes.

Bennu complained the added step delayed her homework from reaching the teachers on time. She expected sympathy. Instead she was told to factor that in and get her homework in early.

All the teachers were required to change their passwords and not post them anywhere students could see them.

Once a week the Kimsara Detective Agency checked each school computer. Rather than report each violation to Vice Principal Dickens, they helped the teachers get their computers secure.

Chapter 19

At Monday's lunch, Emma moaned,"I can't believe the police took the computer hackers to jail."

"They're just kids like us," added Kim.

"My dad said that since they are juveniles they won't get a criminal record," Sara reported. "They're supposed to be back at school tomorrow."

"Aren't we supposed to get our corrected report cards tomorrow?" Kim remembered.

"That's what I heard," Abdi admitted while putting down his cafeteria tray. He produced a letter announcing, "I got a letter from Andy Parta. He's alive." Then he read the letter to the group.

"Wow," exclaimed Sara debating with herself whether to feel guilty since her outburst toward him happened on his last day at school.

Kim knowing her friend added, "Now, don't feel guilty. Thanks to his dad ..."

"He's better off than our computer hackers," Emma finished.

"Are you going to write him back?" nudged Paul.

"Yes," Abdi admitted though not disclosing that he had composed his reply Saturday night after reading the letter. At his mom's suggestion he would reread it tonight before sending it.

"Does he have an email address?" wondered Sara. Then she answered her own question. "I guess he wouldn't if he doesn't have a computer. What's his address?"

All present copied it down with the intention of writing to him. For some it would be the first letter they ever wrote.

That night Abdi reread his letter. After some minor changes he printed and mailed the following:

※

Dear Andy,

I was shocked when I came home from school and got your letter. I've never seen your handwriting before today. I thought about writing back in pen. I started to then made a mistake which I crossed out. I decided it would be faster and easier to read if I typed it.

I will tell everyone at school that you are alive. The rumor went around that your dad killed you. That made Sara really upset. RT asked the principal if they should call the police to make sure you were still alive. The principal said that you are alive and that she has gotten some good reports from your school. I think your letter will kill the rumor. I am glad you are alive. I read your letter to Sara and everyone in the Kimsara Detective Agency. They were happy you had written.

I think you know I am part of that group. We were investigating some missing dogs before you left.

We proved the dogs were not running away but were being stolen. We helped the police find the crooks and put them in jail. We were in the newspaper so I'm including the article with our picture.

Andy, your father did a very nice thing for you. I wish my cousin's father had been like yours. My cousin got serious about the Muslim religion and an old law called the sharia. He accused girls who did not cover their heads or who wore jeans of being evil. When a neighbor kid was caught stealing, he tried to cut off his hand for stealing. He was stopped and went to jail.

When he got out of jail he was even more pushy or radical. Finally, he disappeared.

Months later his family got a call saying Raheem died nobly as a suicide bomber in Iran. His family disagrees and claims the Taliban murdered their son.

I am glad your father stopped you so you wouldn't grow up to be like my cousin, Raheem. I'm not saying you would have become a terrorist. But my cousin used to be fun. He started lots of soccer games when our families got together. He even let the girls play. When he got so serious about religion, he changed. He started pointing out what everyone was doing wrong. He had no time for soccer. Anytime he saw one of the girls playing with us he would yell at her until she ran away crying.

I forgive you. I am happy you are becoming a better person. I hope you will return to our school soon.

Your friend,
Abdi
abdi_a@whistlestop.com

Chapter 20

In Whistlestop that afternoon Marcia, who seldom rode the bus, sat next to Sara in her sister, Kim's, usual spot. Kim had stayed after school for a robotics team meeting.

"Marcia, I'm stunned to see you on the bus. Don't you usually ride to and from school with your mom?"

"Not today. I wanted to talk to you. I'm a good detective," she declared with assurance. "I want to be part of the Kimsara Detective Agency."

"And what mystery do you want to solve?"

"The mystery of the disappearing fire wood?" offered Marcia.

"What disappearing firewood?" pressed Sara keen that Marcia's observations were similar to her own.

"From our woodpile and Emma's, Sue's and Ricky Norton's..."

"And ours," added Sara.

"Yours?"

"I've had this suspicion of wood disappearing. Last Thursday before school I loaded two buckets with wood and left them in the shed. On days like that when Aunt Patty, I mean, Mom, volunteers at the high school to help with the writers club or school newspaper, I try to get the wood. After school I noticed the woodpile seemed lower than when I left it. I took in two buckets expecting to see that Mom had brought in some wood. She hadn't. Before I could ask her about it she came in the door all excited about seeing the deer.

"Excited about deer?" doubted Marcia. "We always see deer. They're as common as ticks in the spring."

"But these are special deer. A doe gave birth in one of our willow patches this spring. So whenever we see a doe with two fawns, we think it's our family of deer. For the first time she saw them close enough to see that their spots have disappeared."

Marcia pulled out a notebook and ripped out a page. "These are all the people who think their wood is being stolen." She had an impressive list of twelve people, several who did not have kids in school.

"How did you find so many people?"

"I heard kids at school say their wood was disappearing. I asked them to check if their neighbors were missing wood. No one is missing a lot of wood, just a half dozen pieces at a time."

The previous weekend Sara had convinced her dad to install the motion detecting camera she had given him for Christmas. He too suspected wood was being stolen. When he got home from work that night they worked on adjusting it. They took turns getting wood while the other one watched what the camera documented. A few adjustments and no one could take a stick of wood without getting caught on camera.

Chapter 21

Sara had previously spray painted the ends of the top layer of wood and then turned the pieces around. She hadn't seen the painted pieces in the wood buckets in the house so suspected they had been stolen. While her scheme proved wood was stolen she didn't expect it to lead to the thief. Yet the next day at school she saw Shawn Nelson walking toward the building with a bucket of wood, several of which had bright pink paint on the end.

"Shawn," she called out, "don't tell me we're heating the school with wood."

"No, Sara, these are for our robot to stack."

"Why the pink paint?"

"I don't know. We don't heat with wood but our neighbor does. She offered the painted ones because she doesn't like burning painted wood."

"Your neighbor?" Sara asked.

"Yeah, Mrs. Gilbert." When Sara didn't register recognition, she continued, "She's the one who delivers the St. Cloud Times. She drives that white Ranger."

"Oh, now I know who you mean. Isn't her husband deployed over in Afghanistan?"

"Right, my mom scolded me for accepting the wood because she probably needs all her wood. It's tough with her husband gone. That's why I go over to her house when I can. She has the cutest two-year-old."

With her mind churning over the information, Sara changed the subject. "Do you think your robot is ready to keep the school's winning streak alive?"

"It's an improvement over last year's."

"Good luck," Sara wished as they parted.

All day Sara mulled over Mrs. Gilbert being the wood thief. It made sense. She stopped by the houses early every day. She turned around in several driveways, including her own.

Then she remembered that the dog thieves said they had been in jail and had a record which kept them from getting real jobs. If she had to go to jail Mrs. Gilbert would lose her job with the paper and her evening job at the gas station. Her mother watched her son while she worked. Would she end up raising him? Would her husband have to leave the National Guard? Was taking a few pieces of firewood enough to lock up a mother and keep her from her baby? Why weren't things black and white?

She wanted to discuss these questions with Kim on the bus. As she boarded it she remembered Kim would be staying after school to work on the robot. She barely noticed when a boy sat down next to her. When he got off the bus with her she asked, "David, is this your bus stop?"

"Yes, though I think you and Kim use it more often. That's my house." He pointed to the house behind them.

"You don't usually ride the bus, do you?"

"No, I usually ride with my dad in the morning and help out at his shop before and after school. However, work has slowed down. Our best salesman died last year so we aren't getting his exotic orders."

"Exotic orders? What kind of business does your father run?"

"We make small parts, specialized nuts, bolts, toggles, stuff like that. Many parts like that are made in China but they take a long time to get to the factories. If their order gets delayed for one reason or another, they'll order enough parts from us so they don't have to stop whatever they're building."

"What exactly do you do?"

"I run whatever machine needs to be run. I am learning to set up and fix some of the machines. If I kept working there Dad wouldn't have enough work for his one full time employee. We had been talking about my working less. Then Mom made the decision easy when she broke her leg. Instead of making parts before and after school, I take care of the chickens for her."

"Sounds exciting," Sara sincerely exclaimed.

David looked at her and realized he did enjoy working with the chickens. Then he inquired, "Are you on another case?" as he pointed to a police car driving toward their house.

"Kind of. Got to go," Sara called back while running home.

Chapter 22

Sara arrived at her doorstep just as Officer Jack Lewis got out of his police car. They greeted each other.

"Are either of your parents home?"

"I'll check," Sara offered. As she opened the door, two dogs bolted out past the officer. She held the door for him to enter.

"Mom," Sara called as her mom walked into the room.

"Officer Lewis," she said while shaking his hand, "what can we do for you?"

"We have had reports of wood being stolen in the neighborhood. Do you know anything about that?"

"We thought we were missing a little wood but weren't sure," Sara immediately offered while panic registered on her face.

"My husband installed a camera to see..."

Sara interrupted, "...if in fact wood was being stolen."

Relief registered on his face as he asked, "Did you catch anyone on camera?"

"They just put it up a few days ago. Sara, have you looked at the video feed, yet?"

"Sorry, I tried pulling it up but ended up deleting it and haven't gotten around to restarting it," she lied.

Patty looked at her daughter and dismissed the officer with, "Once we get it up, if we see something, we'll let you know."

The officer thanked them and handed Patty his card before leaving.

Sara walked out with him and called the dogs back inside.

"Sara, what was that about?" interrogated Patty when she returned.

"I think I know who the thief is and didn't want the video to prove it. I wanted to talk to dad about options because I don't want to get Mrs. Gilbert in trouble with the police if she has other options."

They pulled up the video and watched Mrs. Gilbert take five pieces of wood from their woodpile.

"Five pieces of wood, Mom. Five pieces of wood. Should someone go to jail for taking five pieces of wood?"

"Definitely Art would know," Patty suggested before going to fix dinner.

Sara limped through her homework a bit distracted. Finally her dad came home and over dinner they discussed the wood thief.

"Five pieces of firewood is not a major steal. However, if you take five pieces everyday for the whole winter it becomes a major issue," Art explained.

"Why would she be stealing firewood?" debated Patty.

"To heat her home is my guess. She doesn't make much delivering papers or working at the gas station," Art suggested.

"She'll lose both jobs when the police charge her, won't she?" Sara whimpered. "Isn't there anything we can do to prevent that?"

"You mean without lying to the police?" pushed Art.

"I want to know why she's stealing," Patty declared while entering the gas station's number on her cell phone.

She spoke into the phone, "Will Mrs. Gilbert be working this evening?"

"Yes," a weary voice replied.

"I need to return something to her. I might be in town tonight. If she's working I could bring it with and drop it off."

"I'll let her know. Who should I say is coming?"

"No, don't tell her in case I don't make it to town."

"Road trip," Art declared as Patty put her phone down.

That evening all three drove to town. Patty pumped gas while Art and Sara strode inside. Mrs. Gilbert finished a transaction with a customer who immediately left. She looked up at them.

Sara walked up to the counter and demanded, "Mrs. Gilbert, why are you stealing our firewood?"

She tried to look offended. Then looking down she covered her face in her hand. When she looked up tears glistened in her eyes.

Art handed her his business card. "We have video of you taking wood from our woodpile. The police came by because of reports of wood being stolen in the neighborhood. You are in serious trouble."

He lowered his voice as a woman in Army fatigues walked in and went into the bathroom.

Art continued quietly, "This is not the time or place to discuss this. You need help. I might be able to provide it. Call me." He pointed to his business card.

"I work until eleven tonight. Any chance we could get together tonight?"

The soldier walked up to the counter with a few items as Patty walked in.

Art called, "Patty, want to get coffee with Amy when she finishes work tonight?"

"It's about time we got together," she agreed while Art paid for the gas.

Chapter 23

Sara's thoughts of staying up until her parents returned were quashed as they pulled out of the gas station. Her dad confirmed, "Sorry, Sara, we'll fill you in tomorrow. I'm not sure we'll cover much ground tonight. Do you still have that list of people whose wood is being stolen?"

"Yes, I have it in the notebook I brought along." She pulled it out and handed it to him. "Do you think a lot of people on that list called the police?"

"It just takes one," Art admitted. "Did the police say why they stopped at our house?"

"No," noted Patty.

"They didn't stop at Kim's which is strange since her sister, Marcia is the one who gave me this list."

"Did you tell Kim you thought it was Mrs. Gilbert?" asked Patty.

"No, I didn't tell anyone before talking with Dad."

"You knew it was her before you saw the video. How?" he urged.

Sara explained about the marked wood. When they reached home she finished her homework. Getting ready for bed at her usual time, she wished her parents goodnight and went to sleep. She had forgotten about their rendezvous with Mrs. Gilbert.

As she dressed in the morning, she remembered and asked her mom, "Did Mrs. Gilbert say why she stole the wood?"

"Her husband agreed to fill the woodshed before he deployed. But, he didn't. The wood he had cut down the year before had dried but needed to be split. With her two jobs and caring for the baby she didn't have the time or energy to split it," Patty explained.

"Couldn't she get someone to split it for her?"

"Sara, she felt she was constantly asking people for help when things broke down. She knew that splitting wood was a huge task. If someone split wood for her, she felt she should pay them. She can't afford that. She also can't afford to go through the winter heating with propane. She thought no one would notice."

"She can't give the wood back. Does she have to go to jail?" challenged Sara.

"Art went in early to talk with some of the lawyers about options."

"I thought Dad is an accountant."

"He is an accountant at a law firm. In addition to doing their books he helps on restorative justice and alternative sentencing issues. He thought he might be able to work something out. He needs your help. When we showed her the list of people whose wood was stolen Mrs. Gilbert admitted she didn't know the names of those she stole from. Could you put together a map with all of the places?"

"When does he need it?"

"The sooner, the better," her mom urged.

That morning Kim had gone to school early as the deadline approached for finishing their robot. Her sister, Marcia, already stood at the bus top when Sara approached.

"Marcia, is there some law against both you and Kim riding the same bus?" Sara quipped.

"No, I saw the police at your place yesterday. Was it about the stolen wood?"

"Yes. Did they stop at your house?"

"No. Did you find out more about the thief?"

"I think so. Can you imagine needing firewood so bad you had to steal it?"

"No. There are dead trees all around here that could be cut into firewood."

"Right, if you had a chainsaw and knew how to use it. You would also have to split the wood. Have you ever split wood?"

"No, but I've watched my brothers do it. It's hard work." The girls sat in silence for a few miles until Marcia offered, "If I had to get firewood, I could see taking a few pieces from here or there. That would be easier than cutting down a tree. Isn't that still stealing?"

"Yes, unfortunately it is. My dad is trying to get this person help without going to jail. He needs our help. He needs a map indicating where all the thefts took place. I ran off a copy of the county map and put in the places I know."

"I can put the rest in during study hall today or tonight at the latest."

"Thanks."

They parted. When they met on the bus at the end of the day, Marcia handed Sara the completed map.

Chapter 24

Back in Wisconsin when Andy got Abdi's letter he realized for the first time since moving in with the Quakers that he was happy. Everything in life seemed better, which didn't seem logical. He read the article about the Kimsara Detective Agency and wished he could have been part of it. Then he remembered how he had treated Sara, concluding if he had been back at Whistlestop the old Andy would not have been part of the group.

One evening he asked Quinn if he could write to Sara. Quinn agreed and allowed him to use the computer. That helped since he kept on changing the letter. Finally he had:

Dear Sara,

Thank you for yelling at me when I said those terrible things about the people killed in the Philippines. I am sorry. I was wrong.

I am really sorry for saying your parents were in hell. I am glad you know they are not.

I am living with a church group called Quakers. They don't believe in God the way I did when I lived in Whistlestop. Their God is more like yours, willing to cut people slack, more into loving than sending people to hell.

Since moving here I realized I am a bully. At this school we have bullies who take kids' lunch money and beat kids up. Since I didn't do those things I thought I wasn't a bully. I was wrong. I see I could hurt you by what I said more than if I had beaten you up. I am very sorry for that. Please forgive me.

Congratulations on your detective agency stopping the dog thieves. Abdi sent me the newspaper article with the picture of all of you.

Most of the kids in my homeroom are real poor. One is homeless and lives in his car. We don't have food choices in the cafeteria. Everyone gets the same meal.

Where I live we don't watch TV or play video games. So my life is quite different. I didn't like it at first but I am getting used to it.

Was it hard moving in with your aunt and uncle after your parents died? I thought of you when I first moved here and didn't like it. I am luckier than you because my parents are still alive.

I miss my parents but know I will be going back to them. I hope to be back at Whistlestop next year. I am changing. I like the new me.

Please forgive me for being such an obnoxious bully.

Your friend,
Andy Parta

He gave the letter to Quinn who called Andy's dad for the address. The next morning Andy slipped the letter into the mailbox on the way to school.

Chapter 25

That evening Sara gave her dad the map identifying those whose wood had been stolen.

"Thanks, Sara, this will help when I meet with Amy Gilbert tomorrow. I've got two papers for her to consider. This first one is an apology from her to the people whose wood she stole. The second one is a petition acknowledging that even though Mrs. Amy Gilbert stole their firewood as she delivered the newspaper she should be allowed to continue delivering the paper. She's the first carrier we've had that lasted more than six months."

After reading the papers Sara wondered, "Does this mean she won't go to jail?"

"Unfortunately, I can't guarantee that. A few days after the letter from Amy goes to everyone I'll be sending another letter to them urging them not to press charges. The matter goes away if no one presses charges."

"Do you think everyone will agree to that?"

"So far three people have pressed charges but the police won't tell me who they are. That's why I'm sending the letter."

"Dad, you're not a lawyer, right?" considered Sara.

"I work for a law firm in the accounting department. Since I have an interest in restorative justice the firm lets me help in that field, especially since most of the work is done free of charge. One of the judges really supports restorative justice. I spoke with him and he sees the theft of firewood ideal for the process."

A week later at 7 PM Art stood before a circle of forty people in the large county conference room. "Thank you for coming this evening. You received an invitation because some of your firewood was stolen by Amy Gilbert. Joseph Parta has agreed to be our mediator."

Mr. Parta greeted the group and reminded them: "The action we take holds the same weight as a criminal trial. The accused will explain what she did and why she did it. Then those who wish will have a chance to explain how her theft impacted your life.

"Mrs. Gilbert, you may begin."

After handing her two-year-old to Shawn, who had volunteered to babysit, everyone watched her walk from the back of the room. She stood a wisp over five feet and a bit over a hundred pounds. Her makeup free face looked older than her thirty years. She wore a simple collared white shirt over her dressy jeans. Her notebook contained her well rehearsed speech so she would include what she wanted to say. Art had helped her polish it to be as effective as possible.

Chapter 26

After looking over the whole group she began, "I am sorry for taking your wood. My husband had planned on filling our woodpile before deploying overseas again in September. He's in the National Guard and this is his third deployment. When he's not with the guard he works construction. When he got home from his last deployment most of the crews he worked with were full. He filled in here and there and did some small jobs. He also did a few home repairs for friends. He kept busy.

"In his spare time he cut down some dead trees on our property and helped our neighbors when that windstorm knocked down their trees. He was so busy cutting and stacking that wood he didn't have time to split much of the wood he cut the year before. He would have done more but I kept urging him to spend time with our son. I figured I could split the wood after he left.

"I lied to him and told him I had done a lot of wood splitting before we got together. Honestly, I'm not good at splitting wood. One whack from him and the wood splits. I have to hammer at it forever. So between my two jobs and taking care of our son I didn't get much split before the first cold snap. I saw a lot of full woodpiles when I delivered papers and figured people wouldn't miss a few pieces here and there.

"I was wrong to take it." Her voice trembled as she admitted, "Many of you said you would have given me wood or helped split our wood if only I had asked." She hung her head. "I am so sorry I didn't ask for help."

"Once I started taking it, I couldn't stop. I could never get enough split to get ahead of things. Our backup propane heater cost so much I started using some of the mortgage and food money. I am so embarrassed for myself and my husband. When he found out what I had done he contacted some of his friends and in a weekend they split the wood and filled the woodshed. The solution should have been easy but I couldn't see it. Please forgive me for stealing your wood." Tears streamed down as she returned to her seat.

Chapter 27

Before Joseph Parta reached the microphone a burly man took it. "I'm Jack Becker. Stealing is stealing. If our kids can be hauled off for some computer pranks, a grown women should get serious prison time for stealing our wood."

"Jack, are you referring to hacking the school computer and changing grades at the junior high?" an unidentified woman shouted.

"Yeah."

The woman walked to the mike continuing, "I'm Lucille Arnt. Jack, what our kids did was wrong and a lot more serious than taking a little wood."

"No way," Jack Becker bellowed.

Before Joseph Parta could intervene, Lucille added, "We had some wood stolen. We have plenty and so it has little impact on our lives. None of us are going to freeze to death because we lost a little wood. But grades are important, maybe not as important as high school grades which help kids get into college. What if our kids had not been caught and stopped but continued to do this? What would they hack next?"

Before he could answer, another woman stood up. "I'm Darla Montel." Her voice was barely heard. Someone handed her the microphone. "I agree with Lucy. What our kids did is more serious. Jack, what juvenile detention center is your son in now?" She paused for effect. "None! Our kids could have been locked up. That would have accomplished nothing but eat up our tax dollars. Amy deserves the same break as our kids."

The discussion progressed in that vein until Mr. Porter changed the subject. "Many of us have sons or brothers in their twenties or thirties. After nine eleven they had a choice to enlist or not, right? That's because guys like Chad Gilbert stepped up. They weren't drafted like some of us. Those guys and gals do not have the normal lives our kids have. Multiple deployments are rough on the families in so many ways. So let's give the Gilberts a break and make this go away."

Mr. Parta stood and questioned, "Would anyone else like to speak?"

A man dressed in a business suit stood up. "I'm Luther Anderson, publisher of the St. Cloud Times. At first I wasn't sure why I got an invitation to this restorative justice conference. I have no wood pile. I do, however, have an employee, Mrs. Amy Gilbert who delivers papers for me. Theft is an automatic trigger for firing an employee. When I entered tonight I got a petition signed by over half of you demanding I not fire Mrs. Gilbert or you will cancel your subscriptions. I don't like to be blackmailed.

"Over the years our paper has published many letters to the editor lamenting the growing prison population. Many letters state we imprison too many people, destroying their lives and increasing everyone's tax burden. Many question if we are more interested in vengeance than justice. Some call for compassion as many of you have done tonight. If Mrs. Gilbert doesn't go to jail, I will urge our company to be compassionate and continue her employment." Several people clapped as he sat down.

Mr. Parta addressed the group. "Thank you all for attending this restorative justice conference. The transcript of our discussion will be made available to the county attorney and the judge. If you did not sign in when you entered, please sign in before you leave so you can be sent follow ups from tonight."

Slowly the group dispersed. Within a week all who had pressed charges dropped them, to Amy Gilbert's relief. An editorial appeared in the St. Cloud Times penned by Luther Anderson thanking the town of Whistlestop for using restorative justice as it should be used. Without giving a name he said the process encouraged him to keep a valuable employee who had learned her lesson.

Chapter 28

After seeing so many of his son's classmates at the meeting Joseph ached for his son, Andy. A letter from him to his wife had just arrived and rested in his briefcase. Before turning on the ignition, he called his wife to say goodnight. After Andy left, he had given her an ultimatum to stop being a holier than thou hypocrite and stop drinking. He gave her a choice, divorce him or go to treatment.

Divorce meant she would no longer be shackled to a non-believer. She wanted to divorce him but being a practical woman she did not want to give up the security her husband offered. She wasn't an alcoholic and expected rehab to prove it. It didn't.

The next day Ginger Parta blew up when her husband delivered Andy's letter. She was living in a half-way house. During her treatment not only did she have to give up her drinking she was forced to face her religious radicalism.

After completing the rehab program she needed more support to stay sober. Joseph found his wife a halfway house that would help her keep sober and continue to deal with her religious radicalism. Twice a week he joined her for marriage counseling. While rebellious at first she realized she was pushing her husband, the only man she had loved and who loved her, toward divorce. She stumbled towards honesty, tripping over her anger as she went. Joseph, giving her Andy's letter before their scheduled counseling session put her over the edge.

She lashed out at him in pent up anger before even opening the letter. The counselor constantly urged her to redirect her statements without placing blame. It's hard to stay angry when you're constantly being interrupted. When she finally settled down their time for the session had run out. Without comment, Joseph kissed his wife and left.

Ginger got up to leave but the counselor told her to stay and read the letter. Having been forewarned of the letter, he had cleared his schedule to be with her when she read it. Her husband had not opened the letter so the contents were unknown.

Ginger got up and went to the furthest corner of the room, ripping open the envelop and in the process ripped part of the letter. Her fury grew to a fever pitch when she unfolded Andy's letter. It dissipated as she read. She felt sorry for herself as she read it.

When she finished, the counselor invited her to say how she felt. She prattled through: betrayed by my husband, persecuted for my religious beliefs, not understood, and being embarrassed at what her husband was putting her son through.

When asked what her son was feeling when he wrote the letter she could say nothing. The counselor had moved to the chair next to her, picked up the letter and after receiving her permission read it.

"Does this sound like your son, Ginger?"

"I don't know he never wrote me a letter before." She added a defiant, "He never had to."

Many sessions would center around that letter before she would admit it said her son loved her and appreciated her. In the marriage counseling session she began realizing her husband had feelings and began identifying what they were. Moving from her cloistered, perfect self, to a world where everyone, herself included, had flaws: hurt. A world where people needed each other.

Her first letters to Andy were sent back to her with Quinn highlighting the acceptable parts. Joseph brought the returned letters to family counseling, giving them to her as he kissed her goodbye. She bristled reading each one. She processed each one with her counselor and tried to write another letter. Finally, one went through to her son.

Chapter 29

The next day as Joseph Parta drove to his Whistlestop home from work, he mentally replayed yesterday's call from Andy. He had received a letter from his mother that day. After the usual chit chat, Andy had asked, "May I speak to Mom?"

"Sorry, Son, she's not here." He was regretting this conversation. No matter how often he rehearsed it in his head, he never found the right words.

"When will she be home tonight?"

"She won't be home tonight, Son."

Andy couldn't wrap his head around those words so demanded clarification. "Why not? Did you get a divorce?"

"No."

"Will you be getting a divorce?" Andy considered with some hesitation.

"Why do you ask?"

"Because you two are always yelling at each other. Are you getting divorced?"

"Who can predict the future?" his father answered honestly.

"Dad, what's going on?" Andy demanded, perched on the brink of panic.

"Listen, today is Friday. I'll clear my schedule and come and see you tomorrow. I'll explain everything. Your mother is fine."

"Should I tell Quinn?"

"That would be nice. I wouldn't want anyone to think you're being kidnapped. Ask Quinn what restaurants he would suggest that are near you. Okay?"

"Okay. I miss you, Dad."

"I love you, Son."

When they hung up, Andy didn't know how he felt. Quinn came by to retrieve the phone.

"Did you have a good talk with your dad?"

"Confusing."

"Want to talk about it?"

For the first time since coming to live with the Quakers Andy agreed to talk. Quinn already knew that Andy's father would be coming the next day. But he let Andy tell him how he felt about it. Andy hadn't seen his father in six weeks. Quinn tried to prepare Andy for the roller coaster of emotions he would have the next day.

That night, Joseph Parta, unable to sleep, decided not to wait for morning. He began driving toward his son. He had planned on arriving around lunch time.

He couldn't stop second guessing himself, wondering if he had permanently destroyed his relationship with his son. Phone calls from him at first were filled with anger and insults. Recently Andy had calmed down. He wondered what triggered Andy's sudden interest in his mother.

Deep in thought he occasionally drove over the speed limit allowing him to arrive a little before 8:30 AM. He easily found the dining room where breakfast was winding down. All of a sudden he heard a joyous cry, "Dad you're here," as Andy blitzed out of the dishwashing area.

Giving his father a sincere hug he asked, "Have you had breakfast?"

"That's okay. Nobody should fuss for me."

Knowing his father's habit of skipping breakfast, Andy got a plate, put fruit on it. Then explained, "They have great bread here. This morning there are three kinds."

Quinn walked up naming the three types of bread while shaking Joseph Parta's hand. "You might prefer the quiche," he offered ducking into the kitchen to retrieve what was left.

"It's been years since I had quiche," Joseph acknowledged while Quinn put the remaining quiche on his plate.

Andy returned with a napkin, reporting, "That's really good."

"Hey, dish boy," Melissa yelled from the kitchen. Andy started to get up to return to his kitchen duties. His stomach tensed when she added, "You're fired."

Andy froze and gave Quinn a terrified look. Quinn laughed, "Andy, sit down. That's Melissa's way of saying you don't have to go back and finish your duties. They have enough help. Possibly Arnold took over your duties."

"Whose Arnold?" questioned Joseph.

Before Quinn could offer an explanation Andy enthusiastically acknowledged, "He's a writer. He's working on a mystery book about a kidnapped kid. He's shown me some parts and had me check if the boy talks the way we talk today.

He said it's been a long time since he was a boy and he never had any kids. He was too busy writing."

When Andy took a breath Quinn added, "Mr. Hunt comes here about once a month to ..."

"Refuel in silence." Andy added having caught his breath. "I like it when I sit next to him at dinner. He tells such exciting stories."

"You're not being a nuisance, Son, are you?" asked Joseph.

"He is not. As a matter of fact Arnold seeks Andy out more than vice versa. He says Andy gives him lots of ideas."

"He gives me ideas too, especially when I am stuck on a writing assignment. He'll sign on to a computer and let me use it to type up my story. When I'm done, I print it and give it to him. Then we both sit down and he shows me places that need fixing. He gives me some help if I don't know how to fix it. Dad, I'm getting A's in English. Would you believe it, A's?"

"That's great, Son." He had no trouble believing it because his returned assignments were scanned by Quinn and emailed to Joseph as soon as Andy brought them home.

Joseph put down his fork. Andy immediately bussed the empty dishes to the kitchen and stored the napkin in the guest cubby.

Chapter 30

Joseph stood, saying "Quinn, it's good to see you. Thank you for all you're doing. I'll have him back around noon on Sunday."

When Andy returned he announced, "Come on, Son, let's go for a ride."

Andy joyfully walked next to his dad, both enjoying the unexpected warmth of the November sun. Sliding into the car felt strange. He had become used to Quinn's car with the rips in the seat cover. Noticing the new car smell, he checked, "Dad, did you get a new car?"

"Yes, I forgot you've never ridden in this car."

"But it looks just like you're old car."

"Which worked great so I had no reason not to get the same one again."

"Dad, where are we going?"

"I have no plans, other than being with you. Do you have some suggestions?"

"I want to go somewhere we can talk."

"Okay. First, let's get a place for the night and see if we can check in early?" Uncharacteristically he had not made reservations. Three chain hotels loomed in front of them. "Well, which one should we pick?"

"The La Quinta," Andy suggested. "One of the kid's mom works there. He said they have a great indoor pool. Oh, but I don't have my swimming trunks."

"I packed them for you. So the La Quinta it is." He parked, took out his large suitcase and approached the check-in desk. Andy heard him book a room for two. Satisfied that they could check in right away, they walked toward their room. His father handed him a room key.

When they got to their room, Joseph opened the suitcase and tossed Andy his swimsuit. Then he proposed, "Talk or swim first?"

"Swim," insisted Andy already having slipped into his trunks. He was halfway out the door. He had observed the signs on their way to their room so knew exactly where to go.

Reaching the pool he found he wouldn't be alone. A set of twin boys about his age were swimming laps. Andy began swimming next to them while his father met the boys' parents.

All of a sudden the mother announced, "That's enough," causing the boys to bob upright.

Andy muttered, "What's enough?"

Lars and Lucas introduced themselves and explained that they had been fooling around and messed up their mother's iPhone. She made them do laps until she got it back to the way she wanted it. A hotel employee came by and tossed a ball into the pool. After some discussion the boys played a game of part tag and part water polo which the parents didn't understand.

Chapter 31

"Are you getting hungry?" the boys' father asked.

They paused before answering. Noticing the time on the pool clock, suddenly they were very hungry. Both families met again in the lobby but drove separately to the restaurant with a pirate theme. Quinn had suggested the place because they did entertaining skits while people ate.

The entertainment and tasty meal kept the boys' attention. The adults exchanged the usual background information. Joseph kept his answers sketchy, doing a lot of changing the subject instead of answering questions. They went their separate ways after dinner.

"Nice people," commented Joseph as they settled back into the car. Rain began falling heavy enough to need the wipers.

"If you say so. Lars called his folks bank robbers who had to leave Chicago before they got caught. The two boys were lookouts when they did the robberies."

"They're just pulling your leg. I remember when we were kids on a trip. I told people my dad was the mayor of the town."

"Did people believe you?"

"No, because the first person I told that to happened to be the mayor."

Both laughed.

The rain was getting harder. They decided to return to the motel, shocked at seeing street signs waving in the wind and a garbage can rolling down the street. Joseph quickly parked in a no-parking zone right outside the entrance. As they ran in, tornado sirens sounded. Everyone was told to go to the basement community room.

Joseph was disappointed their talk would be delayed. Then he thought he saw Lars pick a wallet out of a man's pocket. Before he knew it, Andy approached the man asking if he had his wallet. When he realized he didn't Andy walked over to Lars and told him that this was the man whose dropped wallet he had found. Lars tried to deny it until Andy reached into his jacket pocket and retrieved the stolen wallet.

Suddenly, Lars' parents advanced complaining about Andy's stealing from their son's pocket. Then seeing the man with the recovered wallet open it, revealing a law enforcement badge, the family evaporated.

The officer thanked him and offered him a five dollar reward, which he refused. When he returned to the card table, his father wondered, "Son, why wouldn't you take the five dollars?"

"It didn't seem right. I didn't find the wallet. Lars stole it. I just retrieved it." Andy sat in silence rerunning the scene in his head. Then he remembered he had no money. But somehow he survived two months with no money, no TV and no junk food.

Chapter 32

Andy and his father sat down at a card table. As people wandered around the hotel basement a woman approached asking, "Mind if I join you?"

"You're welcome to join us. I'm Joseph Parta. The lad who left to find you a chair is my son, Andy."

He returned with a chair to a surprise greeting, "Hi, Andy. I'm Meg Martin."

Before settling into the chair he carried he shook her hand. His father informed him, "She's a hospital chaplain."

"I was driving by when the tornado sirens blew. I parked in the no parking space right outside the door, and ran in," she explained.

"We did the same," Joseph acknowledged.

The large room easily accommodated the guests and their luggage. Additional tables were set up. Decks of cards were passed around and people began playing cards. Andy offered to teach everyone the card game, Golf, but they decided on Hearts.

As they played talk became comfortable. Before long Joseph realized this woman had led them in a conversation that allowed him to tell his son about his mother's drinking problem. He was surprised that Andy was fully aware of it and expressed relief that she went to rehab.

Then Andy questioned the chaplain, "Do you believe everyone has to declare Jesus as their Lord and Savior in order to go to heaven?

"Do you believe that, Andy?" she countered.

"I used to but I'm not sure anymore. Do you believe it?"

"Absolutely not," the chaplain emphatically proclaimed.

"Why?"

"What made you start questioning what you believed?"

"Coming here."

Joseph curbed his desire to intervene because he wanted to know the answer too.

"My Mom and I used to go to this church that preached everyone who didn't declare Jesus as their Lord and Savior was hell bound. We were responsible to keep as many people as possible out of hell."

"That's a pretty big responsibility."

"I don't know," Andy replied. "I think maybe I liked telling people they were going to hell because it made me feel better than them. Anyway one day we were having current events. Sara, who's in my class, talked about the super typhoon that hit the Philippines and killed 10,000 people.

"I said the people must have really done something bad for God to punish so many people. Sara got angry and told me that God didn't kill those people, that I had a horrible God. She also criticized me for saying her parents were killed in the car crash as punishment for not going to church every Sunday. Then she ran out of the room crying."

"Do you still believe that?" the chaplain pressed.

"No, it can't be. God can't be that mean. I know that now but then I was using religion like a hammer. So that day my dad pulled me out of the public school in Whistlestop and dropped me off with a Quaker friend."

"Was that a surprise?" the chaplain reasoned.

"You can say that again," Andy admitted. "It was like I got beamed to another planet."

"How did your mother feel about you leaving home?"

"I don't know. I haven't seen or talked to her since that day. I did get a letter from her yesterday." He pulled out a well read piece of paper from his jeans. "You can read it if you like."

"Has your father read it?" When both signaled he hadn't, she asked, "Is it okay for me to read it out loud?"

"Yeah."

Chapter 33

The storm blinked the lights in the room off and then on again. The chaplain read:

୶

Dear Precious Andy,
 I love you and miss you. I am sorry you have to face hardships because I wasn't a good parent. I am learning that heaven is wider than what our church preached.
 Thank you so much for writing to me. Please write more and let me know how you are doing.
Love,
Mom

୶

Hearing the words affected Andy more than when he read them to himself.

The chaplain commented, "Sounds like she loves you. Do you miss her?"

"Sometimes. I love my mother, I really do. But she drank a lot and would get crazy. She would yell for no reason or totally ignore what I said to her. I was embarrassed if my friends saw her anywhere except church. She was always sober at church."

His son's understanding amazed Joseph. He added, "Ginger encouraged Andy to take his responsibility for saving other people from hell seriously. To protect Andy from her influence I had to get a restraining order. She can't approach him until she's completed rehab."

The news stung Andy but he wasn't sure why.

"That must be hard on both of you," the chaplain acknowledged as the room plunged into darkness. Cell phones, small flashlights and the room's emergency lights lit patches of the room making it twilight dark.

A hotel employee turned on a powerful flashlight beam announcing, "The storm is over. Several power lines are down including the one servicing the La Quinta. We expect our power to be restored within the hour. Those of you who have not checked in, we will try to help you. Those who are in rooms already will not be able to open your door with your keycard. A staff person can assist you getting into your room. Once the electricity comes on we will need to reprogram all of the key cards.

"Those who are leaving, please be careful of the downed power lines. Several cars in our parking lot sustained damage. Please make sure to fill out insurance paperwork before you leave. Thank you for your patience and cooperation."

"I better be heading out. I just got paged to the hospital," the chaplain announced.

"Thank you for listening. We'll walk you out to your car in case you have any damage," Joseph offered, shining his ever faithful mag light to show the way.

When they got outside, they found their cars undamaged.

Before leaving the chaplain said, "Great to meet you. I'll see you in heaven with God's motley collection of sinners, if not sooner."

Chapter 34

By the time Joseph Parta returned to Whistlestop on Monday he had replayed his visit with his son a dozen times, feeling good about every aspect of it.

Meanwhile Andy's world got stranger. As Andy and Quinn were leaving school Sam Michel rocketed toward them.

"Mr. Quinn, Mr. Quinn, Mama's gone. They're going to tow our home."

Quinn hugged Sam as he began sobbing out unintelligible syllables. "Sam, show us."

Once released he ran down the street with Quinn and Andy keeping pace. Three blocks later they reached an old Chevy Impala. The front and back window were labeled, "Boot and Tow."

"See, my mom's gone. Where is she Quinn?"

Andy noticed scuff marks on the ground and tiny tire tracks. Quinn noticed them too and asked, "Sam, has your mother been sick?"

"She's diabetic. She ran out of her medicine and needed to get more today. This is where I left her this morning. She never parks in the same place when she picks me up."

"Do you have a key to the car?" Quinn asked.

Sam pulled a lanyard from under his worn shirt and handed it to Quinn. He got in and tried to start the car. He explained, "She ran out of gas."

As he tossed a key to Andy he ordered, "Get the gas can from the trunk of our car. Be quick."

Sam rummaged through the back seat. "Oh, no!" he cried, holding up a warn purse. "Mama would never leave without her purse."

Quinn reassured him, "Your mother may have gotten sick and been taken to the hospital."

"Those tracks are probably from the ambulance stretcher," Andy breathlessly added while giving Quinn the car key and spare gas can.

Quinn emptied it into the tank and handed it back to Andy as Arnold Hunt pulled up. He parked his car, took the key from Quinn and said, "I'll park it in my garage. Let me know what's next."

"Thanks, Arnold," Quinn offered while hurrying back to his car. The boys stood stone still until Arnold waved for them to follow Quinn. They ran to catch up.

"Sam, your mother is probably at the hospital. You have her purse. Would she have had a wallet or some i.d. with her?"

Rummaging through the purse, he moaned, "No, everything is here in her purse. Why is that man taking our car?"

"He'll keep it safe. Otherwise it will be towed and you would have a big bill from the impound lot," Quinn explained.

"Where's my mom? How am I going to find her?" Sam wailed.

"Quinn will find her. Won't you Quinn?" Andy assured him.

Chapter 35

"We're going to start at the county hospital," Quinn admitted as he pulled into its parking lot. He walked up to the information desk requesting, "What room is Ava Michel in?"

After a few minutes searching the computer, the volunteer acknowledged, "We don't have anyone here by that name."

"Did you check the emergency room?"

"Yes, sir. We don't have anyone by that first or last name."

Sam began crying. Andy put his arm around him.

Quinn turned to go but then returned to the desk adding, "Would you have a Jane Doe admitted today?"

"Yes." Panic registered in the volunteers face.

"Who can I talk to to see if she is Ava Michel?" The stunned volunteer did nothing. "Could you please call your supervisor and find out who could help us."

"Yes, yes, good idea." After a few moments on the phone he announced, "Someone will be with you shortly."

Before they could sit down a tall man in a gray uniform bearing a security badge approached stating, "I'm Riley Daniels, Director of Security. Are you the ones inquiring about a woman admitted as 'Jane Doe'?"

"Yes, Mr. Daniels, we are," Quinn confirmed.

"Do you have a picture of her?"

"Sam, could you get your mom's drivers license?"

Sam pulled out the purse he had stowed under his jacket. Finding his mother's expired drivers license he handed it to Quinn.

Mr. Daniels took it and scanned it with his phone. He explained, "I'm sending it to the ward to see if it matches the patient we have."

When his phone beeped he confirmed, "She's in intensive care on the second floor." He gave them directions.

"Sam, this may or may not be your mother. I'll go in first to check," Quinn explained as they rode the elevator.

"It's gotta be my mom."

The doors opened to nurses' station. Quinn announced, "We're here to see Ava Michel. I believe you admitted her as a Jane Doe."

"What's your relationship?"

"This is her son, Sam. This is Andy. I'm the guardian."

"The patient is in a diabetic coma. Normally children would not be allowed in but she kept calling for Sam when the paramedics arrived. She slipped into a coma before they could get anymore information."

"Is my mom going to die?"

"We don't expect her to. We have been stabilizing her. She should come out of the coma soon." She lead them into the intensive care unit where the glass outer walls made all the patients visible.

Sam's outburst, "That's my mama," drew everyone's attention. His red face and hand slapped across it demonstrated he knew he should be quiet.

"You'll only be able to see her for a few minutes," the nurse cautioned while opening the door. Sam's mother nestled in a maze of monitors and wires. A tall technician in blue scrubs choreographed the chaos.

"Mama," Sam whimpered as he approached. She moaned. He grabbed her by the shoulders and gently shook her. Quinn reached to stop him but the technician signaled not to. "Mama, it's me, Sam. Wake up."

Her eyes fluttered open. She smiled. Responding to her waking up, several people entered the room. "Sammie, I'm sorry," she murmured.

"Mama, you're going to get better. You gotta get better." Tears streamed from his eyes as he laid his head down on her shoulder.

"I will Sammie, I will," she whispered.

Chapter 36

A nurse approached and stated, "Mrs. Michel, you are in the hospital. You have been in a diabetic coma. While we examine you, your family will be waiting in the room just outside this door."

Quinn tapped Sam on the shoulder. He kissed his mom and left with the others. They were directed to a small room. A woman joined them introducing herself. "I'm Nicole Miller, a hospital social worker. You're the patient's family, right?"

"Ava Michel," Quinn offered.

"Thank you. You're Ava Michel's family."

"I'm her son. How did my mom get here?" Sam asked.

"Did you know your mother was a diabetic?"

"Yes, and she ran out of her medicine yesterday."

"Do you know what medicines she's taking?"

Sam dug through his mother's purse and pulled out several empty pill bottles. He handed them to her.

"Is this your home address on these medications?"

"Not anymore," Sam muttered.

"What is your address?"

"Our car."

"Sam and his mother are homeless," Quinn explained.

"Sir, what is your relationship to the patient?"

"A friend and the guardian of her son," he claimed while taking a worn paper from his wallet. Ava Michel had signed it two years ago giving him guardianship over Sam if she ever became incapacitated. He handed it to her.

She looked at Andy and asked, "Are you his brother?"

"No, just a friend. I live with Quinn," Andy explained while nodding his head in Quinn's direction.

"Sam, your mother was walking erratically in the street. Someone saw her and got her to a park bench and called 911. She wasn't making any sense. Did she have breakfast this morning?"

"No, she was saving to buy her medicine."

"Does she skip meals a lot?"

"Yes, ma'am. Money's been tight because they cut her hours at work."

"Where does she work?"

"I don't know. The places keep changing."

Quinn added, "Last year she worked through Manpower but I thought she had found permanent work."

After looking at the paper Quinn had given her she asked, "May I copy this for her file?"

"Yes," Quinn agreed.

"Could you fill out the paperwork for her? None was done when she came in."

Quinn surprised the boys with, "No, Ava's awake. You need to get the information from her."

After she left, a nurse knocked on the door and entered announcing, "Mrs. Michel is asking to see her son." They stood and followed him back. She was sitting up. All but one of the monitors were turned off.

"Good news. I'm getting out of intensive care," Sam's mother exclaimed.

Quinn looked at her sternly. "Ava, you are not leaving this hospital until your doctor discharges you."

"Quinn, I know. Will you take care of Sam until I am on my feet?"

"I wouldn't have offered if I didn't mean it. One of his classmates, Andy Parta, is living with us. So he won't be alone."

"Andy, are you the one who has been helping my Sammie with his math?"

"Yes, ma'am."

"Thank you." Then she turned to her son. "Sammie, I'm so sorry. They probably towed our car away because of my parking tickets." Tears filled her eyes.

"No, Mrs. Michel, Arnold Hunt is keeping it safe in his garage until you need it," Andy volunteered.

"Arnold Hunt?"

Andy explained, "He's a friend of Quinn's. He's my friend too."

"Your car will be safe. Do you need anything from it?" Quinn asked.

"Just my purse," she said. Her son passed it to her. "Thanks, dear."

"Mom, can I stay here with you?"

"No, I'm afraid not. You go with Quinn and you mind him."

"Say goodbye to your mother, Sam. We need to head home for supper. Ava, he'll be back tomorrow during visiting hours."

Quinn led Andy out of he room, giving Sam a few minutes alone with his mother.

Chapter 37

The week flew as Sam and Andy balanced school, visits to the hospital and homework. Sam's mother improved steadily. On Friday as they entered the hospital, Sam stopped and greeted a woman waiting near the door, "Aunt Violet, hi."

She introduced herself to the others. "I'm Violet Johnson, Ava's sister."

"She lives in Minnesota, Elk... something," added Sam.

"River, I live in Elk River. My sister, Ava is being discharged today."

Sam clapped. "Quinn, can she live with us?"

"No," his aunt firmly stated. "I'm taking her home with me to Elk River."

"Me too?"

"No, Sam. Your mother and I decided it would be best if you stayed here and finished the school year. She needs to rest and know you are taken care of. She trusts Quinn more than she trusts herself right now. I know this is hard but your mother can't take care of you now. She'll be coming down to say goodbye before we leave."

"Today?" Sam's voice quivered and eyes teared.

"Yes, Sam, she should be down shortly." She handed him a tissue.

Quinn ushered him into a nearby restroom and had him run cold water over his face. He planned to give him a pep talk.

After drying his face, Sam spoke. "I know my mom needs help. If I stay with you she won't worry about me. I'll miss her."

They walked out as Ava Michel was wheeled toward them.

Sam straightened his back then walked to his mom. He kissed her. "Mom, you look so much better. I'm glad you're going to Aunt Violet's for a while. I hope you don't mind. I will miss you. But can I stay with Quinn and Andy for a little longer and finish school?"

Tears streamed down his mother's face. "I'll miss you too. I'll work hard at getting better so we can be together soon."

Sam noticed his Aunt Violet had driven the car to the door. The nurse let him wheel his mother out and assist her into the car. Tearful goodbyes were exchanged.

After a silent trip home, Andy helped settle Sam in their room. A surprise letter from Sara Cowley perched on the dresser. He immediately ripped it open:

༺

Dear Andy,

    Thank you for your letter. I felt guilty about getting you kicked out of school. Thanks for saying that it is making you a better person. I hope you will be able to return to Whistlestop.

Our Kimsara Detective Agency is trying to help a woman who was stealing wood not to go to jail or lose her job.

Do you have any mysteries we could work on? We could use a big project. February is always a boring month.

Hope to hear from you again,

Your friend,
Sara Cowley

※

"Good letter?" Quinn questioned.

"Yeah it's from a friend in Whistlestop, Sara Cowley." He handed it to Quinn who read it and handed it back.

"Is she part of that detective agency you talked about?" asked Sam.

Andy confirmed it with a nod as Melissa strode by reminding them to hurry if they wanted dinner.

Chapter 38

The next day as Quinn, Andy and Sam were playing Chinese Checkers, Andy asked of no one in particular, "What can we do to help Sam's Mom?"

"My mom needs money, lots of it," Sam confessed.

"Why?" Andy innocently inquired. He regretted asking when he saw the shocked look on Quinn's face.

"The last time my mom got sick, she lost her job and couldn't pay the rent. We got evicted. Because we got evicted no one else would rent us a place. So we've been living in the car. She got a lot of parking tickets because she couldn't pay the parking fees near some of the places she worked. She has a lot of doctors' bills to pay too."

"Maybe we could shovel sidewalks or get a paper route and earn some money to help your mom," Andy offered.

"While its a good idea, you would need to get your father's approval. This isn't the safest of neighborhoods," Quinn noted.

"Okay, Quinn. May I call my father tonight?"

"Andy, you can call your father anytime you wish. Didn't you put your phone in your top drawer when your father gave it back to you? Or, have you lost it at school?"

"I wouldn't trust taking it to school. Since Sam just won the game, okay if I go and call him now?" He returned the marbles to the board before getting his phone.

As Andy expected his father did not want him shoveling snow or delivering papers. Rather than wallowing in disappointment, he headed to the library. Then he turned back to his room remembering his father had returned his laptop. He wrote,

Dear Sara,

Thanks for your letter.
I don't have any mysteries for KDA to solve but I sure could use your help. One of my friends has a mother who needs a lot of money. His name is Sam and he is living with me now because his mother is too sick to take care of him. We wanted to help her by shoveling snow or delivering papers but my dad says the neighborhood is not safe enough for us to do that.

Do you think KDA could help by doing a bake sale or something? She needs lots of money. They don't have a home. They have been living in their car and have a lot of bills.

Anything KDA could raise would really help.
I'll be home for spring break. See you then.

Your friend,
Andy

Just then Quinn walked into the room. He asked, "Are you emailing your friend?" Sam joined them.

"I hadn't thought of that. I planned on mailing her."

Quinn pulled out a cable from one of his drawers and handed it to Andy who attached his tablet to the wall jack. Then he realized, "I don't have her email address."

"Do you have anyone from Whistlestop's address?" proposed Quinn.

"Not anyone in my class."

"What about that Ab...Ab...something who wrote to you? Didn't he have his email address at the end of his letter?" suggested Sam.

"Yes, Abdi did." Andy pulled out the letter, grateful for Sam's observation. He emailed his letter to Abdi asking him to send it to Sara.

When Abdi received it he forwarded it to Sara and all the members of Kimsara.

Chapter 39

The next day the Kimsara Detective Agency gathered for lunch bantering about raising money. Many had given serious thought to the venture. Conner wanted to organize a 5K run. Paul thought he could get his father to do a taco benefit after the run.

Emma proposed, "We could have an auction. My cousin, Heather, is planning the Whistlestop Charity Auction for the last Saturday in April. While the majority of the money raised goes for the United Way other charities can benefit and get 80% of what their items raise. She offered to add a few items especially if we have some quality jewelry or something like that to donate."

Paul asked, "What happens with the other 20%?"

"Ten percent goes to the United Way and ten percent covers the cost of the auction," Emma reported. Her cousin had prepared her for such questions which made Emma feel confident promoting the auction.

"I have a fancy necklace, I could donate," Sara offered.

"You mean the one that you wore in the picture in the newspaper?" Only Kim and her immediate family knew she found it in a secret closet with a note from her birthfather.

"Yes, Kim, that one."

"Are you sure?"

"Yes, I feel uncomfortable wearing it. Mom took it to a jeweler. They appraised it at $50,000. So we put it in the safe deposit box."

Emma expressed everyone's awe, "Wow, no wonder you don't wear it."

"That piece alone could pay a lot of rent for Sam and his mother," noted Kim.

"Even though it's worth $50,000, unless we get a lot of people bidding things can go for less than they are worth. Last year I think the highest item was a boat which sold for $9,000," Emma admitted.

"That was a beauty, a Skeeter Bass Boat worth a lot more. My dad didn't know about it before the auction or he would have bid on it. We've got to do more advertising than last year," RT insisted.

"I'll tell my cousin about the necklace. I'll check with my mom and see if she has a piece of jewelry to donate," Emma offered.

"Why don't we all check? Emma, will your cousin need to see the jewelry or would a picture do?" inquired Sara.

"For now, let's stick with pictures. The better the picture the more likely, it'll be featured in the advertising," suggested Emma.

The next day at lunch Emma gathered two dozen pictures for her cousin.

Conner working at his usual do-it-yesterday speed passed out flyers for a 5K run which he titled "Running to End

Homelessness, one family at a time." He had already found sponsors to donate t-shirts and checked with the mayor about the route. He challenged, "Does anyone know when the snow will melt?"

"August, is a sure bet," quipped Abdi.

"Seriously, I think we would be safe to have it April 15th," suggested Paul.

"Bad day," Kim stated. "Taxes are due that day."

"How about the Saturday after tax day?" proposed Sara.

They all agreed on the day.

"The auction will be the week after that. So we could advertise the auction at the run," Emma added.

"I'll get some letters to the editor written," Abdi offered.

Chapter 40

That night Abdi put together his master letter:

∞

Dear Editor:

KIMSARA (Kids In Modern Schools: Aware, Responsible, Active) has adopted a homeless family and invites the community's assistance.

A single mother was raising her son, paying her bills and living in an apartment. Then she got sick but didn't have medical insurance. She lost her job and apartment. She has been paying a little on her medical bills from temporary jobs when she can get them. She and her son lived in their car until she got sick and ended up in the hospital. This time she has insurance to help pay her bills.

She is recuperating at her sister's tiny apartment in Elk River. Her son is living with friends. She hopes to move back to our area.

She won't have a job until she gets well. Kimsara is hoping to raise enough money so the mother and son can live together. We have recruited some volunteers to help the family get their finances organized. The mother has refused to declare bankruptcy.

After you file your taxes on April 15th, please join us in helping this family. That Saturday there will be a 5K "Run to End Homelessness, One Family at a Time" beginning at 8:00 A.M. in the high school parking lot. The next Saturday, several items on the annual Whistlestop Charity auction are dedicated to helping this family. Finally, donations can be made through the Whistlestop Credit Union. More details can be found at Kimsara.com.

Thanks for your help.

Abdi Ibraham
Kimsara Member
Whistlestop Junior High

❧

Abdi emailed the letter to the Kimsara regulars. He immediately got three emails and four tweets encouraging him to go ahead and send it out. He sent it to five newspapers, varying each one slightly. He also encouraged everyone to post the information on their Facebook pages and email friends. RT put the information on the Kimsara web site.

Sara immediately made an entry to Facebook. Her brother, Jerry surprised her with a call a few minutes later.

"Sis, you could use some help on your fund raising, right?" he teased.

"What kind of help?" Sara cautiously countered.

Chapter 41

Her brother continued as she prepared for bed, "Marketing majors need to create an ad campaign. One of them might be interested in working one up for the Kimsara fund raising."

Beginning to understand her brother Sara reasoned, "Would you happen to have someone in mind?"

"Yes, his name is Adam Otto and he's sitting next to me. Adam, meet my sister, Sara," he said as he passed him the phone.

"Hi, Sara. I need to prepare an ad campaign by next week. The one I've been working on one is falling apart. It sounds like you have a lot of fund raising going on in the next couple of weeks. I could take what you have and get professional looking flyers. I could also get some media coverage."

"Editorials are being sent to the newspapers," Sara reported.

"Could we meet, soon?" Adam suggested. Putting the phone on speaker, he handed it back to Jerry.

"Sara, could you and some of your friends meet with him after school tomorrow?" Jerry proposed.

"Where?"

"Just in case you'd agree, I called the school this afternoon and the principal offered the cafeteria as a meeting place. I explained that I wasn't sure if this whole thing would work out. She needs to know in the morning if you need the space. So is it a go?" Jerry pushed.

"I'll check with the others and let you know," Sara replied.

"And Sara," Adam added, "encourage them to bring any pictures they may have of the auction items. Do you have pictures of the family you are helping?"

"No, that could be a problem," Sara admitted.

"Why?"

"They live in Wisconsin. At least Sam does right now. His mom is living in Elk River."

"I've got to go. I have an evening class. If you could write down how your group picked this family, it might help," Adam offered. "See you tomorrow after school. Here's Jerry."

"Thanks, Sis, I got to go too. See you tomorrow. Say hi to the folks for me. Bye."

Sara felt a bit dazed. She emailed everyone connected with Kimsara.

⚘

Re: fund raising
My brother has a friend who is willing to do publicity for our fund raising. He would like to meet with us after school tomorrow in the cafeteria. Everyone who

can is welcome to join the meeting. Please bring copies of anything you have already done and any pictures you have that could be used in publicity. Also, bring ideas for flyers. See you then.

Sara

Chapter 42

Sara went downstairs where her parents were playing cribbage. "Jerry says hi," she announced.

"He phoned? Actually talked, not a text message?" gasped her dad in shock.

"Yes. You know this fund raising Kimsara is doing?"

"For Andy's friend?" her mother clarified.

"Yes, Jerry has a friend in advertising who needs to do an ad campaign and offered to do it on our fund raising."

"That's great," her dad burst out. His wife kicked him from under the table. He looked more closely at their daughter. "You look like you have some reservations."

"He wants pictures of Sam and his mother. We were doing this kind of secretly, not letting them know until we gave them the money."

"Are you thinking they might be uncomfortable openly asking for financial help?" her mother suggested.

"That and...," Sara pondered for the right words. "Lots of fundraisers emphasize how the money helps the local community. These people live in Wisconsin. If we advertise that, will people want to give? Also, if people want to know how we picked the family, do we tell them about Andy?"

"I see your problem. Sara, if you take my place, I'll make a few calls. I want to get some advice on how to spin this." Seeing his daughter's knit brows he added, "I'm just getting some facts that you and the rest of Kimsara can use."

Sara sat down and finished the cribbage game with her mother. They heard her father in the background on the phone. After the game Sara went to finish her homework. Thoughts of the ad campaign kept distracting her.

"I may have something." Her father's words startled her. She turned and looked at him standing in the doorway with a notebook in his hand. "When you get an email from Andy Parta, bring it downstairs and we'll try to put it all together."

"No," Sara challenged. "Let's talk about what you have now."

"Okay, but let's do it at the kitchen table where we can spread out."

Sara had a sinking feeling that the fund raising was being taken over by her parents. That had happened so many times in the past. She felt defeated and almost tripped over the dogs waiting for her at the bottom of the steps. Seeing them she realized that would've happened in the past with her parents who died in the accident. Her new parents were different. At least she hoped they were.

Her mother poised at the table with paper and a marker asked, "Okay, Art, what did you find out?"

"First, Sara, you won't get any pictures of the people you are helping. I spoke with Mrs. Michel. She's embarrassed that money is being raised for her and Sam. She is also grateful. She is originally from this area and is ashamed to admit she hasn't made much of her life. She is thinking of returning to the area. She has no reason to move back to Wisconsin."

"She got sick. Do you know what she has?" Sara inquired.

"Quinn told me she has diabetes but doesn't publicly acknowledge that. She's always been thin and so it took some time before she got an accurate diagnosis. Quinn is going to talk to her and see if she would let the fund raising highlight the need for doctors to realize skinny people can have diabetes. Until Mrs. Michel approves, no mention can be made of her medical condition."

Chapter 43

Sara's phone pinged, announcing a new email with a Quaker address. "That must be the email from Andy you expected, Dad. I'll go print it." She bounded upstairs and printed three copies without reading it. She returned and passed out the copies. All read:

≈

Sara,

I talked with your dad and my dad and Quinn. Thanks for doing the fund raisers. It would be embarrassing for Sam and his mom to use their names or pictures. Would people in Whistlestop care about one homeless family in Wisconsin. Advertising for the fundraising is hard. Isn't it?

Perhaps you could use this:
I am Andy Parta. I used to go to Whistlestop school. I was a bully. I didn't know it until my dad took

me out of school and made me live with a friend of his in Wisconsin. I used to think that my religion was the only religion and was mean to those who did not believe like I did. I have found out that God is bigger than my idea of God. I'm sorry I put down other people's idea of God.

There is a kid in my school who was living in his car with his mother. They have no home. They lost their apartment when his mom got sick. She had a disease that obese people get so it took a while for them to figure out what she had because she is normal size. She is still paying off her bills from that time. Recently she got sick again and had to go to the hospital. Her son is living with me until she gets better. They want to move back to Minnesota.

When my Whistlestop classmates found out about my friend and his mom they agreed to have a fund raiser to help them out.

Thank you, Kimsara, for helping them out. Thanks also to all who will help out with their fund raisers.

Your friend,
Andy

Tell your dad that my dad read this letter and said it was okay to use it.

꽃

"That should help out. Shouldn't it?" Sara hoped.
"Andy must really want to help these people out," her mother realized.

"Sara, that looks like it's the only thing you have for your meeting tomorrow," her father added.

"Thanks, Dad, for getting that."

Before going to bed Sara sent a copy of Andy's letter to everyone in Kimsara. They never used it.

Chapter 44

The next day after school as Sara approached the cafeteria, her phone rang. She didn't recognize the phone number. "Hello, this is Sara Cowley."

"Sara, I'm Avis Michel. My son, Sam is a friend of Andy Parta who said you were doing a fund raiser for us."

"Yes."

"First, thank you. Second, Quinn has convinced me that in your advertising you could make people aware of the type of diabetes I have. It's called TOFI for 'thin on the outside, fat on the inside.' Those of us who are not over weight often don't get our diabetes diagnosis right away. Our high glucose readings are dismissed as a fluke that should be watched but not taken seriously. For me it took a major hospitalization to get doctors to treat me as a diabetic.

"I'm sorry I am not comfortable with using my name. It's embarrassing to ask for money. But I thank you for what you are doing."

Sara had entered the cafeteria and pulled out a piece of paper. She wrote as she spoke. "That's TOIF diabetes, Mrs. Michel?"

"That right, Sara. Thanks for your help."

"You're welcome."

Adam and Jerry were already at a table introducing themselves to the Kimsara regulars. Sara arrived last. Adam stood up and moved in front of the easel he had set up. He addressed the group, "I'm Adam Otto a marketing major. I need to put together a marketing campaign and understand you are trying to organize a fund raiser. Let's start with identifying the purpose of the fund raiser. Why do you want to raise money?"

"To help a homeless boy and his mother so they don't have to live in their car," offered Conner.

"Do you plan on raising enough money to buy them a house?"

"That would be nice but we won't raise nearly enough," Peter admitted.

"How much do you plan on raising?" questioned Adam.

"As much as we can. Why do we have to have a target amount?" countered Sara.

"Having a goal is often a good motivator. What if we set your goal at $10,000?" Adam's question generated groans.

"Wait," Kim cautioned. "If we add up the run and auction, we might be able to make that amount."

"Okay," Adam agreed as he wrote the amount on the first sheet of paper. "What do you expect this would buy?"

"A couple month's rent," offered Emma.

"Paying off some medical bills," declared Sara.

"Letting them live together again," added Peter.

As suggestions were made Adam wrote them down. Then he flipped the paper over and wrote on the clean sheet: Why give?

Suggestions flew from the group. He wrote: People like to help. Everyone needs a home. Kids should live with their folks.

"Wait," RT cautioned. "There are a lot of nameless, homeless people out there. These people don't want us to use their names, which is a problem."

"But if we use their names, people might not give because these people live in Wisconsin," explained Emma.

"Having pictures and names of real people is effective in drawing people to a fund raiser," Adam conceded.

Chapter 45

"What about a disease? Would people be more willing to support fund raisers to end a disease than to help one family get housing?" Since no one responded, Sara continued. "I just got off the phone with Sam's mother. She has diabetes but doctors didn't check her for it because she wasn't overweight. It's called TOFI and means 'thin on the outside but fat on the inside.' She thinks more people should know it exists."

Conner admitted,"I'm debating about canceling our run because there is one already scheduled for that day: Step Out to Stop Diabetes."

"Let's put it on hold for now. I have a contact organizing that run and I'll see if you can work something out with them," suggested Adam.

"Abdi's letters to the editor already call the 5K a run to end homelessness. Isn't it too late to change it?" questioned Conner.

"No," admitted Abdi. "Our fund raisers are six weeks out. The papers wouldn't print the editorials until closer to the date. So I could send in some changes if I did it soon."

"Would two days from now be enough time?" proposed Adam.

"That should work," agreed Abdi.

Adam continued, "About the auction, I know your town has an auction every year. Ten percent of the price goes to the United Way, ten percent toward expenses and the person owning the items gets eighty per cent. Your group has collected a number of items for the auction. Do I have that right?"

"Yes," everyone agreed.

"These are pictures of the items that will be donated," Emma explained while handing him copies of the pictures she received.

"Anything else?" Adam looked around the group.

Peter met his eyes and finally admitted, "My Dad offered to donate 10% of his profits from our Mexican restaurant on the day of the run or auction."

"Does the restaurant have a big screen TV?" Adam asked.

"Yes, we usually have it out for soccer games, nothing else."

"That's good to know," Adam said. "Does anyone have sketches for any flyers?"

"I do but they're for the ending homelessness run," admitted Conner.

"May I have them?"

Conner handed them to Adam, who then said, "I'll work on these ideas and see you the day after tomorrow, same time, same place."

Two days later the Kimsara group gathered. "Anybody know where Adam is?" canvassed Conner as his phone rang. "Adam, where are you?"

Conner put his phone on speaker so everyone heard, "I can't make it but I've worked up a power point presentation. Any chance I could email it to someone?"

RT spoke up. "You can email it to me at RTwithIT@whistlestop.net."

"Will do. Conner, thanks for putting your phone number on your drawings. I did speak with Whistlestop Designs about the 100 shirts they were donating. When I explained... I guess I should start at the beginning.

"The Diabetes 5K risked canceling their run because of lack of interest. They are willing to merge with you and share the profits since you are helping. Highlighting TOFI type of diabetes sounded good to them, especially when I told them some med students would be willing to help them out."

"Power point is loaded," announced RT.

"You should be looking at the flyer for the run. I used Conner's art, changing the wording and adding the American Diabetes Association logo. What do you think?"

"Sharp, great," were among the positive comments called out.

Adam continued, "Next is the entry form for the 5K run. It's the same as the original one for the Diabetes Association, except on the bottom you have the banner with TOFI awareness. Any entries submitted on this form will be credited to the Kimsara fund raising effort. So make sure you have people use this form."

"I'll get the form on the Kimsara website and make some copies we can pass out," offered RT.

"I'll keep you informed," Adam promised before ending the call.

Chapter 46

The unseasonably warm February and March buzzed with activity. The fundraisers had been planned for April. As part of his project Adam had prepared public service announcements for every radio, television and internet messaging service in the area. He identified who should receive the announcements and when they should be sent.

The Kimsara Detective Agency had nothing to do but wait, which suited Sara. She enjoyed the extra time playing with the dogs and challenging Kim at computer games.
One morning Sara flew out of the house catching up with Kim as she crossed the street to where David stood watching them approach.
Kim's mischievously addressed David with, "Well, you finally got the dress code right." That drew him from his revery. Finally he noticed all three were dressed in grey hoodies, kaki shorts and sneakers. Before he could find a clever reply, the school bus stopped for them.
David had been thinking that seventh grade had become the year of the couple. The three year tradition of

soccer lunch banter with his band of buddies died. As boys merged girls between them their flirting, giggling, texting had totally changing the lunch time experience.

While Dave had always liked girls, he rejected narrowing his world to one other person. Recently he started welcoming two seventh grade classmates to his bus stop. They crossed the street to get choice seats which would not be available when the bus returned to pick up their side of the street.

David liked them, especially Sara. While the girls were friendly, Kim and Sara were often deep in conversation. Their talk of a dog theft ring had drawn some of his friends to join them for lunch and skip their quick soccer game. Since no one would steal his pit bull, Daisy, he preferred soccer.

Chapter 47

David couldn't believe Sara and Kim were serious detectives, though he had to admit they found the dog thieves. As he thought about spending more time with Sara, inspiration struck. On Friday morning while waiting for the bus he asked, "Would either of you be interested in learning more about chickens. I could use some help."

Kim quickly replied, "Yuck, chickens are messy and mean."

Sara looked thoughtfully optimistic but remained silent.

That night when they got off the bus, Sara asked David, "Are you serious about helping with the chickens?"

"Yes, you interested?"

"I know nothing about chickens but would love to learn. When can I start?"

"In about a half hour, after you change into dirty clothes. I mean clothes you don't mind getting dirty."

"I'll see you in a half hour in my gardening gear." So an after school routine of laughing over chicken antics began.

Chickens bonded them. Two weeks later when Mrs. Clemens down the road decided to move to an apartment, she offered David her eleven hens and one rooster. David knew their layer coop was full and the broiler coop would be too big. So as they got off the bus one afternoon, he offered Sara and Kim some chickens. He explained he had been offered a dozen more.

Kim rolled her eyes and hurried home, throwing back, "Keep them on your side of the street."

Sara however checked, "You really don't want them?"

"We don't have room for them. I promised Mrs. Clemens I would find a good home for them. Are you interested?"

"I am, but want to be sure. We'd need to build a chicken coop, right?"

"Not necessarily. Mr. C. talked about getting chickens a couple of years ago. You've got that coop on the other side of the drainage ditch. That would be too big. Did you know that little white shed near the pole barn used to be a chicken coop before your parents bought the place?"

"Really?" The two were deep in conversation as they crossed the street and approached Sara's house.

Sara's father stepped one foot out the door and into David's question, "Mr. C. are you still interested in getting some chickens?"

Totally caught off guard he looked from Sara's eager face to David's. Something was up. "Why, do you have some extras?"

"Not exactly. Mrs. Clemens is looking for someone to take her chickens when she moves to an apartment. She doesn't want to butcher them because they're young and just started laying eggs."

"How much does she want for them?"

"Nothing much, just a few eggs now and then."

"Oh, Dad, please. We could put them in that white shed with all the junk in it."

"Sara, you want chickens? If we take them they will be your chickens."

"Yes, yes, I'll take care of them."

"You'll have to get the shed ready for them," her dad stated.

"I'll help Sara, Mr. C," David offered.

Sara's mother drove up, rolled down her window while assessing the excited group. "Mom, we're getting chickens." Seeing her father's backup expression she added, "That's if it's okay with you."

"I'd love to have the fresh eggs. These are layers, right?"

"Right, Mrs. Clemens' little flock," David explained.

"Art, I thought chickens would be too much work. What's up?"

"These will be Sara's chickens. She'll be cleaning out the white shed for them."

"With my help," David repeated.

Chapter 48

That weekend as winter returned David got quality time with Sara. They spread tarps over the fresh snow and began emptying the shed onto them. One bag of trash, a pile of scrap metal, some lumber and a huge box labeled "chickens" sprawled before them. After some debate, they brushed down the cobwebs, swept the floor and washed the whole place including the windows, grateful they had found rubber gloves big enough to go over their gloves.

As they started opening the big box barking dogs announced the arrival of Jerry. Sara called out, "Brother, we could have used your help earlier."

"Timing, Sis. I have that gift. Hi, Dave." A further look and he wanted to know, "Don't tell me Dad is finally getting chickens."

"No, I'm getting chickens," Sara proclaimed.

"Do you know anything about raising chickens?" Jerry prodded.

"Just what I've learned from David."

"And I'll be around to help," David volunteered.

"What are you going to do with all the scrap metal?" Jerry quizzed assessing the pile.

"Jerry, I would say from that look in your eyes, you have some ideas," Sara claimed.

"I do. I'll be right back."

Jerry headed to the house while David began pulling treasures from the box: a three gallon plastic waterer, a galvanized feeder, and some heat lamps.

As Sara pulled out a fruitcake tin, pointed to the label, asking, "What's grit?"

"Rocks that chickens use to help them digest their food. Our chickens find enough stones. We use it when we get a batch of day old chicks and put a little out in the winter."

Sara closed the tin and placed it on the tarp.

David grunted, "Sara, help me lift this wooden box out. It's really forced in there."

After the two tried for awhile, Sara suggested, "Let's put the box on its side." Then she peeled off the tape sealing the box bottom. Pulling the flaps open, she righted the box and lifted the cardboard off the wooden box.

"Nesting boxes," cheered David as he turned it over. "I'll bet those holes match the pegs on the wall."

The two lifted the box in place. They hung the heat lamps and plugged them in. "Looks like we are ready for the chickens," Sara said.

"Not quite. Just to be on the safe side, let's paint the place with barn lime to make sure it's sanitized. I'll go get some from home," Dave offered while turning to go.

"Deserting my sister already?" Jerry accused as he approached.

"I'm just getting..."

"I'm teasing, David. But before you go, could you please help me load all the scrap metal into my trunk?"

As the two began loading, Sara joined them, grateful they let her and didn't have her stand aside just because she was a girl.

Sara's dad called out, "Lunch. Jerry and David join us, please." After putting the last of the metal in the trunk, they washed up to share a pizza.

Chapter 49

By suppertime the warmed chicken coop had been brushed down with barn lime and set up ready to go. David had brought a bucket of feed back with the lime and brushes. They were admiring their work when Jerry returned.

"Good, you're ready for the chickens I brought you."

David's eyes registered panic. "No, it has to dry for at least a day." Looking at Jerry's smirk he added, "Wait, you didn't bring us any chickens did you?"

"No, I forgot them." He gave Sara a handful of money.

"What's this?"

"Chicken feed. I cashed in the metal at the recycling place. Now you have money for chicken feed."

Sara hugged her brother. The three admired the coop before going their separate ways. On Tuesday evening, Mrs. Clemens came in her son's pickup to drop off her twelve precious chickens, her leftover feed and all her chicken supplies. While she had wanted to check the place out before bringing her chicks, she accepted David's word that it would meet her standards. It exceeded them.

Every day Sara and David talked chickens before or after school. Both were comfortable with their non-dating relationship. They helped each other with their chicken duties. Often they invited each other to join a non-chicken group activity.

On the bus David usually sat near Kim and Sara. The day after Sara got her flock, Kim surprised him by passing Sara and going to the back of the bus.

"May I sit here?" he asked with hesitation.

"Sure."

"You and Kim aren't sitting together?" His voice had an under-shadow wondering if they had had a fight.

Picking up on his concern Sara laughed. "While we usually sit together, Kim is sitting with Pat so they can plan out their science project for next year. They'll build on what they did this year." Talk turned to chickens.

They hadn't noticed the bus had stopped until Kim came by announcing, "I'm so excited about our science project,"

Sara stood and followed her.

Kim turned and challenged her, "Have you found a partner yet?"

"No. Kim, the project is due next October. What's the rush?"

"Research, we need time for research. See you after school."

Witnessing the exchange, David began hatching a plot. He needed to move fast but not too fast.

After school Kim again sat with Pat and Sara with David. "Kim is sure excited about her project. Sara, do you remember what they did?"

"David, I'm surprised you don't remember. Name the most dynamic project at this year's science fair."

"The drone. Was that Kim and Pat's project?"

"Yes and they have made a lot of improvements on it since then."

"Do you have a science project partner for next year?" My partner from this year moved to Texas. Our project was lame," David admitted.

"No, I don't. Do you think we could do one on chickens?"

"Sure, but do you have any specific angle for approaching it, Sara?"

"No, but let's keep a running list of possibilities. We have time before school lets out if we want to get it okayed before summer break."

"So, it's agreed. We'll be science project partners next year."

"It's agreed." Sara extended her hand so they could shake on their arrangement. Both left the bus with a spring in their step.

The next morning while waiting for the bus, they agreed to call their project: "The Life of the Chicken." During study hall David put together a very generic outline and emailed it to Sara across the computer lab. Sara waved at David who had been looking for her reaction. Her thumbs up sealed the deal so he forwarded the email to Mr. Olson, the science fair director.

That evening as she got on the bus, Sara checked her emails. She handed David her phone as he sat down. He read the email from Mr. Olson accepting their project.

They high-fived.

Chapter 50

The next day in Whistlestop every possible shade of green exited the school announcing school spirit day to the unknowing. Being March, green was the chosen color. The sky even wore a green hue.

"Are you adopted?" a sad sixth grader dressed in olive green asked hunter green Sara as she sat down on the bench next to her.

"No." For the first time in her life she faced this question. Realizing it was no longer true she added, "Wait, I guess I am because my aunt and uncle became my parents when my biological parents died." She pondered the why of the question.

"You're the detective, Sara, aren't you?" the girl mumbled.

"Yes, but I don't know who you are?"

"I'm Mary Smith and I just found out I'm adopted. Can you detectives help me find out who my real parents are?"

"You mean your biological parents," Sara clarified.

"Whatever," Mary moaned.

"Did you ask your parents, the ones you are living with, who your birth parents are?"

"No. They don't know I know I was adopted."

"How did you find out?"

"Last night my mom told some one on the phone that she regretted waiting so long to tell me that she wasn't my mother and didn't know how to do it now."

"Wow. Are you sure she was talking about you?"

A dejected, "Yeah," had Mary on the verge of tears. She squinted her eyes, swallowed hard and continued, "They have been lying to me all these years. All of a sudden I don't know who I am. If I asked them, can I trust they'll tell me the truth?"

Mary's shocked disorientation stunned Sara. "Wow," was all she could say as her own problems dimmed.

"Sara, can you help me find my parents?" pleaded Mary bringing Sara back to the present.

"Maybe we could help you. Do you look like your parents?" As she offered this she realized that she herself did not look like her current parents. She herself looked adopted.

"I'm the only one in the family with brown eyes. Everyone else has blue or green eyes."

A car pulled up in front of the school. "Got to go," Mary announced while gathering her things.

"My mom's right behind yours," Sara said as she joined the race to the awaiting cars. She missed something Mary mumbled as she glanced at the woman picking up Mary.

Sara got in the car, greeting, "Hi, Mom. Thanks for picking me up." Then she totally confusing her mother as she buckled her seatbelt muttering, "That's not her mother. She had brown eyes." Sara went on to explain her conversation with Mary.

"Mom, somehow I don't think it would be right for us to help her find her real parents, but I'm not sure why?" Sara confessed.

"How is this different from other tasks your group has handled?" her mom prodded.

"This is more personal. There could be something her parents want to hide from her."

"Your mean some sinister reason for her being put up for adoption?" her mother suggested.

"Yes, or maybe she had been stolen as a baby," Sara dramatically added.

"I doubt if it would be such a made for TV story," her mother claimed. "She just found out yesterday, right?"

"Right."

"So you might be the first person she's told."

"But I've never spoken to her before. Why would she tell me?"

"Pretty much the whole school knows you and Kim. So when she gets time alone with a known detective she had the courage to admit being adopted."

"I don't know what to do next."

"Sara, I would wait for her to approach you again. Maybe saying it to you, a stranger, would give her the courage to say it to her family. Hopefully, she has some relative she could talk to if she needs to work up courage to ask her parents.

Chapter 51

Meanwhile, Mary had greeted her aunt/godmother, Josie, who arrived for their monthly get together.

"So your friend thought I was your mother."

"Yes, her mother was picking her up." Then feeling a surge of courage she asked the adult she trusted most, "Am I adopted?"

"That's complicated."

"No, it's not. I'm adopted or I'm not adopted. What's the problem?" Mary demanded.

"I'll explain but not while I'm driving. I picked up some subs for a picnic." They both observed the green sky with dark clouds sliding over the sun. "I picked them up in picnic perfect weather."

"But mother nature looks like she wants to cry," Mary observed wanting to cry herself.

"So we'll go to my place in duck perfect weather," Josie countered while putting on the wipers to fend off the rain.

A crack of lightening and the drum of dropping rain deadened further conversation. Once at the trailer park they wordlessly waited for the torrent to subside a little. When it did, they ran from the car. Mary took the short cut jumping over the wooden ducks on the lawn.

Once inside they fell into the familiar routine of getting supper together. For as long as Mary could remember at least once a month they got together for dinner and a sleepover. Mary even had her own room in the elegant trailer.

The table set, drinks poured and the meal unwrapped, they sat down. As Mary turned "Wheel of Fortune" on, Josie felt relieved. Quickly they blessed their food and guessed the first puzzle.

They ate while basking in guessing most of the puzzles before the contestants. The winner of the final puzzle won the million dollar jackpot. As confetti fell, Josie took the win as a good omen. She turned off the TV while they cleared the table.

"Let's sit in the living room, Mary."

"Will you tell me if I am adopted?"

"Yes. Though I am not sure where to begin. Have you ever seen your birth certificate?"

"I don't think so," Mary mused.

"I have a copy of it," Josie admitted while pulling out a scrap book. Mary sat next to her examining the document on the first page.

"That's my birth certificate? So I'm not adopted," Mary hoped.

Josie remained silent while pulling out a second birth certificate stored behind the first.

Mary observed, "This one is different. They both have my name and birthdate. They can't both be real can they?"

Then without pausing for a response she added, "This one has your name on it. Why?"

"Because I gave birth to you."

Chapter 52

"You? You're my mother?" Mary exclaimed in shock.

"I carried you in my womb but my sister has been your mother. She raised you. I got pregnant when I was sixteen. The captain of the football team had asked me out on a date. My friends warned me not to go. But he acted like he really cared about me. When I told him I didn't want any beer, he got me a root beer. I think he put something in it. We went farther than I wanted to but I was too out of it to tell him to stop."

"So he raped you."

"We didn't think of it as rape back then. Boys got away with it. The girl got blamed for letting it happen. So I didn't say anything about it. Three months later I told my older sister, your mom, that I had been missing my periods. She took me to the doctor who confirmed I was pregnant."

"Was grandma mad when you told her?"

"I never told her. Your mom had been married about a year. They were moving to Chicago for jobs and to take care of your father's grandmother. I wasn't doing very well in high school despite your mother's help. I was always fighting with our parents. So your mom convinced our parents to let me move with them to Chicago. I would go to the high school where your mother would be teaching. She would help me with my homework. I would help take care of Great Grandma Mitchell. We left in June and I didn't return until the next June."

"You didn't go home for Christmas?"

"No, my brother-in-law as the newest doctor working at the hospital had to work that holiday. Our dad planned to drive up for the holidays. Then he broke his leg and couldn't drive and our mom didn't like driving long distances."

"What did they say when they found out you were pregnant?"

"They never found out, as far as I know. The original plan had been to put you up for adoption. When Great Grandma Mitchell found out about it, she suggested it would be better if your mother acted like she had had the baby. They wanted kids and hadn't had any luck getting pregnant. By that time I was pretty attached to you growing inside of me and couldn't see giving you up for adoption. So the idea of keeping you in the family appealed.

"I never understood how the original birth certificate got changed. I know my brother-in-law, your father, and the priest who baptized you had something to do with it."

Mary scrutinized the two documents. "Why isn't my father's name on this one? It says 'unknown.' Why?"

"He didn't know he had fathered you. I didn't want anything to do with him, especially not share you with the jerk," Josie admitted.

"Do I know him?"

"No, he died in a motorcycle accident two years after you were born."

Chapter 53

The doorbell rang. Josie went to answer it letting in a torrent of rain and two men carrying empty boxes. "Ray," she exclaimed in surprise as she kissed her best friend.

"You know my neighbor, Brian," he noted while bracing himself for Mary's combination tackle and hug. "The weather's bad. After I picked up Brian from work, I decided to pick the two of you up and take you home with me. There's a tornado watch until midnight. You know, Josie, you are not safe here. Use these boxes. Pack what you can.

Ray lined the bottom of one box with the throw from the couch and told Brian, "Get as many things from the walls and tables as you can carefully packed into this box."

Josie found Ray uncharacteristically overdramatic. She wanted to chide him but didn't because his hunches were usually dead on.

The phone rang. Josie grabbed it cutting off the caller with, "We're heading for shelter. I'll have Mary call you when we get settled." She hung up.

Ray expecting Mary's parents on the call offered, "I'll help Mary. You get your things. I have my truck so we have plenty of room."

Ray found Mary in her room with a dresser drawer open, holding the empty box.

"Pack as much as you can," he ordered as he scooped her shoes and everything else from the closet floor into her clothes basket. He reached over to the drawer and pulled everything out, tossing it into the box Mary held. "Quickly get as much as you can," he repeated, grateful that she began emptying the other drawers. He collected all of the hangers with everything on them, added a picture from the wall and hurried out with the filled basket.

Brian had filled his box and checked, "This goes in the truck, right?"

"No, put it in the car. Get as much in the car as you can. Then come back for this basket," which he set down by the door.

Josie joined him with a box holding her laptop some CDs and books. Mary followed with her filled box topped off with her stuffed skunk and pillow. Ray took the box from Josie admonishing her to, "Get your pillow and nightclothes while I put this in the car. Mary, is that box too heavy?"

"No," she admitted while following him to the car. He helped her settle her things. Seeing Josie coming he insisted, "Both of you get in the car and drive to my place. Be careful. I'll lock up. Josie, drive into the garage." He kissed her as he tossed her bundle into the back seat. Brian closed the trunk after settling Mary's backpack next to the filled clothes basket.

Both men raced back into the house. As planned they each took a laundry basket. Ray tossed a bath towel to Brian for the bottom and told him to put in everything from the kitchen cabinets he could manage. Ray filled his with laundry detergent and cleaning supplies. After tossing them in the truck they returned for a few small pieces of furniture. Within five minutes they were locking up and heading out the drive.

Ray dropped Brian home just as the tornado sirens sounded. He was grateful to see Josie's car already in the garage and the door opened for him to park next to it. He turned off the engine as the garage door shut and the door to the kitchen opened. The three hurried to the basement where Josie had already lit the lanterns. The weather channel updated them on the approaching tornado.

Chapter 54

Outside the wind howled. Everything went black, except for the lanterns. Both Josie and Ray witnessed the terror in Mary's face. Mary realizing they were staring at her, tried to think of something to say when her phone rang.

"We're fine, Mom. We're safe in Aunt Josie's boyfriend's basement. We already made up the couch for us to sleep on."

"I'll be fine." She handed the phone to Josie saying, "Mom wants to talk to..." She mouthed the final word, "Mom."

Mary blocked out the conversation. A nerf ball hurled toward her. She caught it and pitched it at Ray who had moved into a dark corner. They pummeled each other until Josie called a truce with, "Mary, say good night to your folks."

She did, looking Josie straight in the eye as she said, "Goodnight, Mom. I love you."

"Anyone for a movie?" suggested Jay.

"Jay, be realistic, we don't have any power," Josie admonished.

"But, Aunt Josie, your laptop runs on batteries."

"So does mine," said Jay as he scrolled through a list of movies.

Mary looking over his shoulder suggested, "Kung Fu Panda II. Can we watch that? I wanted to see it but somehow never got to it. Uncle Jay, you wouldn't mind watching a kids movie, would you? Please?" Her puppy dog face was hard to deny.

He felt like laughing but instead changed the subject. "If I'm uncle and she's aunt, does that mean..."

"It means I'm not comfortable calling you "Ray" and I don't remember your last name. Besides, she's my mom but you're not my dad," Mary mocked.

"Too deep, too deep. We'll watch it," he surrendered.

As the movie started Ray pulled out some still cold beverages from the basement fridge. Things had quieted down outside so he grabbed the flashlight and scouted some snacks from the kitchen. He came back reporting, "The storm is dying down. The block is dark but looks pretty much intact. Did I miss anything important?"

Since both responded, "No," Ray settled in to be bored. "Wait a minute, a panda is being raised by a stork?"

"Allegory, Love, think allegory," sighed Josie.

"Now I know why my parents didn't want me to see this movie." Neither adult pushed for a further explanation. Noting Ray's confusion Mary continued, "I'm adopted." Then she questioned her own statement, "I am adopted, right?" She looked in her aunt's eyes for confirmation.

Instead she got, "Well, technically, you've never been officially adopted."

"So I am your daughter and am being raised by your sister as her daughter."

"That's correct."

Ray already knew the secret. He wanted to leave the room but instead just concentrated on the movie.

"That's why I have two birth certificates. Neither is 100% correct."

"True."

Silently they continued watching the computer screen. Mary's world made more sense than a stork raising a panda. She felt ambivalent about her godmother being her birth mother. She wondered if her life would have been different if she had known sooner. Her exhaustion yielded to sleep as Kung Fu Panda said, "You gotta let go of that stuff from the past 'cause it just doesn't matter. The only thing that matters is what you choose to be now."

Jay gradually lowered the sound while Josie pulled off Mary's shoes and settled her head on her pillow. They went upstairs with the laptop. Ray found a news channel and saw Josie's trailer park being scanned. Many trailers had been leveled. Noting a bedraggled lilac bush on the edge of an empty concrete pad, Jay wondered, "Isn't that your lilac bush?"

"Oh, my God. Jay, you saved my life and my daughter's." She let his arms enfold her as she cried.

Chapter 55

The tornado that struck on Friday night in the Whistlestop Trailer Park destroyed three trailer homes and heavily damaging several others. No residents were injured.

The TV news reports showed the wind damage throughout the area. "We really lucked out," Kim told Sara as they watched. While branches were strewn all about their properties, what they saw on the screen was far worse.

As the cameras panned the trailer park, Sara pointed to the screen, exclaiming, "I know her. That's Mary Smith. She's in sixth grade."

"She looks pretty calm for losing everything she owns. So does her mom," Kim commented. "I would be crying my eyes out if our home was destroyed like that."

Sara had not told anyone except her mother about her conversation with Mary. Her mother joined them commenting, "Maybe not. You might be in shock so you wouldn't register any emotion. You would just be relieved that you are alive."

Sara's father joined them. He set the newspaper on the coffee table open to the second page with pictures of the storm damage. "Looks like Kimsara made the paper." He pointed to a small article to the side of the storm damage one.

"Ouch," winced Sara's mother.

"What's wrong Mrs. C?" asked Kim as everyone huddled over the paper.

After skimming the article Sara questioned, "Mom, do you think people will be less likely to help out with our fundraisers since it is helping someone from out of state when people in our town just lost their homes?"

"That may be," her mom admitted.

Both Kim and Sara took out their phones and began reading texts from many in the Kimsara network suggesting they should expand their fundraising to include the storm victims. Neither texted a reply.

Finally Kim grumbled, "If we include all the storm victims, will the money we raise help Andy's friend and his mom very much?"

"In a way by putting the article on your fundraising next to the storm damage pictures, the editors highlight the fact that your cause is not local. So expect questions to be raised," Sara's dad proposed.

"What should we do about it, Mr. C?"

"Wait. Go ahead with your plans. Don't rule out sharing the proceeds but don't commit to sharing them," he suggested.

On the way to church the next day they saw lots of storm damage. They weren't surprised that a collection for the storm victims was taken. One of the families who lost their trailer were members of the church and had been taken in by an elderly woman who lived alone in a huge house.

The next day at breakfast Sara's dad gave her the newspaper telling her, "Check out the editorials. But don't let anyone from your group respond, at least not for a couple of days. Let others weigh in first."

Sara took the paper, ran to catch her bus, opening the paper as she sat down.

Chapter 56

At the bus stop David and Kim's discussion of the editorials ended as both Sara and the bus approached. Neither said anything until Sara finished reading:

Wake Up, Kids

Kids in Whistlestop are so concerned about one family that doesn't live in the community they are raising money for them. This Kimsara group should realize their neighbors are more important. They should redirect any money they raise to help the storm victims. If they don't everyone should boycott their fundraising events.

V.P. Dickens

"That's a pretty strong letter," David noted from across the aisle when he saw Sara had finished reading it. "What are you going to do about it?"

"We should write our own letter back. Right, Sara?"

"Not yet, Kim. Dad suggested we wait and see what others say. By then we should know what to say," declared Sara.

"Isn't the writer the vice principal?" David noticed.

"You're right. I didn't catch that," Sara admitted.

They continued their conversation at lunch where many Kimsara regulars had a variety of opinions.

"Do you think the vice principle wrote the letter to put the Kimsara Detective Agency in a bad light?" RT pondered

"Why would he do that?" challenged Kim.

"Well, first of all the article in the paper didn't mention the auction or run as Kimsara events. Also, he wasn't all that happy that we figured out who hacked the school computers and changed the grades," RT explained.

"School computers he was supposed to keep secure," added Kim.

All ate quietly until Emma realized, "Doesn't his brother live in the trailer park? Maybe he knows his brother needs help."

"I agree we should wait before we comment. The more people who comment, the more publicity we get for our fundraising," declared Abdi.

"But what if everyone boycotts us," pouted Kim.

"They won't. Trust me they won't," assured Abdi.

The next day six editorials addressed the fundraising. Four said only local needs should be considered. One suggested V.P. Dickens meant people should only help his relatives who lived in the trailer park and only had minor damage to their uninsured trailer. The final one was the best:

Storm Relief

Whistlestop is a generous community which should not be bullied into boycotting a few students from helping someone outside the community. If you go to the town website, you will see how you can help the storm victims.

A generous, anonymous benefactor has agreed to match all of the donations the students receive, dollar for dollar, up to a half a million dollars. The money will go to the tornado relief fund so all the money the students raise can go toward its original purpose.

Joseph Parta, JSD
for an anonymous client

&

At lunch the Kimsara regulars discussed the editorials.

"Do you think Andy's dad is the one who is giving the money?" Abdi proposed.

"No, definitely not." Sara was firm as she continued, "I got an email from Andy saying his father had been approached by one of his clients to match the money we raise. Andy suggested he mention we weren't going to be bullied into changing course."

"We got fifteen registrations for the Diabetes Run, a one day high, the day the editorial on boycotting the run appeared," Conner reported. "Part of that could have been the article explaining the run appearing the day before, but we can't say for sure. We now have 70 people signed up and still have three weeks before the race."

As the bell rang ending lunch Sara sighed, "Can you imagine if we could raise a half a million dollars?"

"That's a bit above our $10,000 goal which now seems reachable," Kim added.

Chapter 57

On the bus ride home Sara and David discussed how lucky they were that the storm did not disturb their chicken coops.

David asked, "Have your chickens started laying eggs yet?"

"I got my first one the day of the tornado. It was olive green. Is it spoiled?"

David laughed. "No, you have a few Araucanas. They lay colored eggs."

"Do they lay a different color every day?" wondered Kim who was no longer totally avoiding the chickens since Sara spent so much time with them.

"No, I'm pretty sure each chicken lays the same color all the time," David explained.

"As soon as I figure out who laid the egg I'll name her Olive." Sara changed the subject with, "David, how's your mom doing?"

"She got her cast off and is moving around better but doesn't want to go into the chicken coop until she can wear her rubber boots."

"If I were her I would make sure the boots never fit," quipped Kim as the three got off the bus.

They were greeted by a rush of chickens. "How did your chickens get out?" grumbled Kim as she hurried away from them.

"Mom must have gotten home early and let them out. Don't worry they won't follow you home. Daisy trained them not to cross the road," David kidded as Kim walked across the street backwards to make sure.

"Is it too late for me to let my chickens out?" debated Sara.

"Time isn't as important as what you are letting them out into. Let's go check."

David dropped his backpack inside the porch door, thanked his mom for letting the chickens out, grabbed his boots and headed with Sara across the street. When they arrived he said, "The dirt around your coop is pretty dry, so I would let them out."

She opened the door, surprised that the chickens readily swooped out.

David cautioned, "You probably want to bring your dogs out on a leash until you know if they'd chase the chickens."

"Good point," said Sara. "I'll be right back." She returned with their two leashed dogs. She had changed her shoes for rubber boots. The dogs, barking frantically, lunged towards the chickens nearly dragging Sara behind them.

"They might be barking at me," admitted David as he walked away from the coop. They followed him. "Maybe they're protecting your chickens from me. Is this the first time you've let them out?"

"No, the dogs were out this morning."

"No, I meant the chickens," clarified David.

Sara blushed. "Yes, this is the first time the chickens have been out of my coop."

"Do you usually let the dogs out after school?"

"Usually."

"Do you just open the door or put them on leashes?"

"It depends. If I am going to take them for a walk, they're on leashes. Otherwise not."

"Then let's take them on a walk," David suggested holding out his hand for one of the leashes.

Sara gave him Mitzy's leash considering, "Won't Daisy get jealous."

"Not if we pick her up on our way."

Sara wasn't sure it would be wise to have all three dogs together but decided to see what would happen. They walked over to David's house. He handed her Mitzy's leash and went into the house. He opened the door holding a leash while Daisy plowed past him barking passionately. David whistled. She instantly quieted and sat down at attention. David praised her while attaching her leash.

Mitzy and Max stood at attention next to Sara who held their leashes close to her.

David walked a few steps closer to Sara while explaining to his dog that they were friends. Sara moved closer following David's signal. When the dogs were closer, and their tails wagged their leashes were lengthened. The three dogs mingled, sniffing each other out.

They walked away from their houses for about ten minutes. Then David proposed, "Since the dogs seem to get along, I'd like to go back to your house. We have them on leashes let's see how they do with the chickens."

"All three of them?"

"Sara, trust me. We can handle this."

They approached the coop angling away from it as far as possible. The chickens kept picking at the grass. "My dogs seem more interested in keeping your dog away from the chickens than anything else," Sara observed.

"They're smart. I only let both Daisy and the chickens out at the same time when I am there to keep an eye on her. I don't trust my dog alone with chickens. After I leave you might want to bring your dogs out one at a time and see how they handle the chickens." David turned to go. "See you tomorrow, Sara."

"Wait, how do I get the chickens back in the coop?"

"They'll go in automatically by dusk. If they don't call me."

"Don't worry. I will," Sara declared as she took her dogs into the house.

Chapter 58

That evening after supper Sara went outside and found all twelve chickens roosting in the coop as David had predicted. The dogs had come out with her but showed no interest in the chickens. She closed the coop. Since she finished her homework before dinner she headed in and sat down joining her parents watching TV. Her father asked her, "Have you heard from Andy Parta lately?"

"No, should I have?" Sara wondered if her father knew something she didn't.

"He is coming to town for spring break, isn't he?"

"Right." She scrolled through her emails on her phone and decided to go to her room and open them on her computer. Most of her communication these days was done through text messages. Unopened emails were a low priority that she would tackle tonight.

After deleting the ads, she found one from Andy which read:

Our spring break starts before yours does. My dad is going to pick me up early. I had hoped I could come to school for a day or two. We have been talking about me returning to Whistlestop after spring break. I am afraid I have gotten behind since our school is different than yours. I don't know if I would fit in any more.

Sam will be coming with me. He and his mom would like to thank everyone at school for their help. My dad is arranging something with the principal. Abdi has been sending me information on your fundraisers for Sam and his mom.

Good luck with the fundraisers and thanks for helping my friend.

Andy

꧁

Sara printed the email so she could show her dad and take it to school. After many rewrites she replied with:

꧁

It will be good to see you, Andy. When I came out of a coma I didn't want to go back to school because I was afraid I would never catch up. It took a while for my brain to remember words and things.

But I caught up. That was at my other school. The kids there weren't as friendly as the ones in Whistlestop. So, I don't think you'll have any problem catching up. We'll all help you. And you don't have a brain injury like I had.

I saw your mom and dad at the high school play last weekend. They sure looked happy. They would probably like having you back home. So I hope you do stay.

Your friend,
Sara

☙

Andy's phone pinged. He was getting used to having it back. When he saw it was from Sara he scrolled through the message. The words, "mom and dad," prompted him to call home. His mother answered.

"Mom, you're back home?" Andy exclaimed.

"Yes, Andy, I am so looking forward to seeing you on spring break."

"You sound happy, Mom."

"I am. I am," she repeated relishing the realization. "Your father and I had grown apart over the years, in part because of my drinking. Now we're starting over and it feels great."

Andy felt a deep desire to be back home.

"Joe, Andy's on the phone. Do you want to speak with him?"

"Sure. Andy, how's it going?"

Andy thought he heard a kiss as the phone was exchanged. "Okay, Dad. Mom's home."

"Yes, she is and she is looking forward to seeing you. How's school going? I'll put you on speaker so your mother can hear too."

They discussed school. All were in agreement Andy should finish the year in Whistlestop.

Before hanging up his father added, "I've been talking to Quinn and Sam's mom. Would it be okay if Sam also came and stayed with us until his mom got a place for them?"

"Yes, Sam could share my bedroom and his mom could stay in the spare room," Andy offered.

"His mom wants to stay with her sister until they have a home of their own," his mother explained.

"Okay."

"Your friends are very seriously fundraising to help make that happen. They have signs all over town," his mom said.

Andy got an inspiration. He asked, "Do we have to wait for spring break? If we came sooner, we could help with the fund raising."

"I hadn't thought of that. Let me check it out and get back to you, Son."

"Thanks, Dad. Good night, Mom and Dad, I love you."

Chapter 59

Meanwhile, Sara had gone downstairs handing her father the email. "How did you know I was getting an email from Andy?"

"I didn't. His dad and I have been working with Sam's mom to get her finances in order. She has an unbelieveable amount of medical bills."

"How much money will she need to pay them off?"

"More than you kids can raise. We're trying to get some of the debt forgiven. She should really declare bankruptcy. However, she won't. She also doesn't want to use the money you raise for the medical bills. That money she wants dedicated to housing."

Sara returned to her computer and checked the online auction site. In a week the auction would begin. Twenty items, including her necklace had been donated and were marked with a magnifying glass, which had become the symbol for the Kimsara Detective Agency.

Then she checked on that weekend's diabetes run. A team of Whistlestop athletes were running but most associated with Kimsara were providing support with registration and along the route. Sara and Kim were passing out water at the halfway point while both sets of their parents were helping direct traffic. Registration had closed when they got their 100th registrations. A day later it was reopened noting that last minute registrants would not get an official T-shirt. One hundred and fifteen were now registered.

Monetary prizes had been donated by the local Lions and Rotary Clubs in several categories encouraging more runners.

At lunch the next day the Kimsara regulars gathered. Emma asked, "Does anyone know of a place that doesn't have signs for the run and auction?"

"No," exclaimed Kim. "I think Adam got ads to every business."

"Jerry said that he got an A on his project. He is so grateful we let him do the advertising he got all his friends to make and post signs." Sara continued, "They put them in St. Cloud, Elk River, Becker, Princeton and dozens of other cities."

"I've seen them in some Facebook postings and blogs," noted Emma. "I wish I had a brother like yours, Sara."

"Did everyone who volunteered to help get an email with directions?" checked Conner.

Everyone had.

"Conner, are you doing the run?" questioned Sara.

"When they added a prize for the first wheel chair to finish, I had to. Since that wasn't listed as a category when we started I don't think I'll have much competition. Last month when I got home from school I found someone had dropped off a racing wheel chair with my name on it. I've been doing some practicing. I might be the only one it that category."

"What about Gary Johnson that veteran who almost won the Big Lake Spud Fest Run last year? He was in a wheelchair and was in the top ten with the regular runners," Abdi reminded.

"Thanks, Abdi, for the reality check. I'm still going to try. This is my first competition. You've got to start somewhere."

Chapter 60

On Friday classes were shortened to accommodate a final assembly. Several reporters and one TV station were present. As students settled in the gym, the principal began, "I would like to present, Mandy Clemens the chair of the diabetes run who has asked to address you."

"Thank you, Principal Jones. As many of you know this weekend is the annual diabetes run. We were about to cancel it for lack of interest when Conner Clemens approached us about combining their fundraising with ours. I think he's part of the Kimsara Detective Agency who wanted to help a homeless woman in Wisconsin. She suffers from a form of diabetes known as TOIF. Will those who are part of Kimsara, please stand?"

As most began standing, Principal Jones, interrupted while motioning the children to sit, "While it started as a detective agency, Kimsara is more of a movement that includes all the students willing to do their civic duty to be a positive influence in the world."

"Thank you for the clarification. I do understand that students from this school are responsible for recruiting a college student to advertise the event. Also, that many of the students are volunteering to help with the race. I wanted to thank all of you.

"I would now like to introduce, Mrs. Michel who is one of the people who will benefit from the run." A slim woman approached the mike while buttoning her navy blazer.

She looked down at the clip board she held and began reading, "I will forever be grateful for your interest. I had diabetes for several years before it got properly diagnosed. Many think if you have diabetes you should be overweight. I have never been. So my doctors kept dismissing my borderline sugar levels and I kept on getting sicker. Getting sick is very expensive, especially before we had health insurance. Doctors aren't doing that anymore. But..."

She looked up away from her text and began again. "I have a son who is in seventh grade, about your age. Can you imagine how I felt when the bills got so overwhelming, I couldn't pay my rent? I was too sick to work at times so I lost my good job and could only get temporary work on days I felt well." She teared up a little, wiped her eyes with her hand and continued.

"Things got so bad we were evicted from our apartment and lived in the car. I don't want you to feel sorry for me. A lot of people have it much worse. I am here because some of you heard of our problems and decided to help us. I am so grateful for that." She motioned to the sidelines. "That's my son, Sam. Thanks to what you will be doing this weekend, we have the hope of living together again. Thank you."

Chapter 61

The principal took the mike. "I am so proud of the students from this school for reaching out like you're doing.

"We have one final speaker, a former student who has something to say."

Some students gasped as Andy Parta approached the mike. He held the speech Arnold helped him write.

"Thank you, Principal Jones. As many of you know, I am Andy Parta. When I went to this school I was a bully. I didn't think I was because I never beat anyone up, but I sure put people down. I am sorry, please forgive me.

"The dictionary defines a bully as: 'a blustering, quarrelsome, overbearing person who habitually badgers and intimidates smaller or weaker people.' That was me. I felt I knew how to get to heaven and anyone who didn't do what I did was going to hell. As a result I didn't have many friends. My dad tried to tell me I was wrong, but I didn't listen to him because I figured he was going to hell. My dad was afraid I was going to grow up to be a Christian terrorist, if there is such a thing.

"Anyway, my dad loved me so much and knew I needed to change. So he kicked me out of the house."

Some students gasped others giggled. When they settled, Andy continued. "Not really, he just sent me to live somewhere else so I could see life differently.

"I lived with people who didn't care what I believed. They believe in a God who is bigger than all religions. They believe that helping your neighbor or even a stranger was more important than how often you went to church. They go to church almost every day for some quiet time with God.

"I went to a school where most of the kids got free lunch and breakfast. For some of the students those were the only meals they could count on. Everybody ate the same food. We didn't have choices like you do here.

"I met Sam at school. If you're living in a car like he was, you go to gas stations or fast food places to wash up; but only if you have enough gas to drive there. Last night I had running water for a shower and to brush my teeth. I've always had that.

"In my months away from Whistlestop I've realized how privileged I am and how much I've taken for granted. I also realized I had been a bully. When I wrote to some of the kids here who I had bullied, they forgave me. Not only that so many of you have been working hard to help Sam and his mom. Thank you. Have a great run on Saturday and I look forward to returning here for school."

The students began clapping just as the bell rang. The principal called for silence and dismissed everyone in the usual order.

Chapter 62

Saturday morning the Diabetes 5K fundraiser began promptly at 8 AM at the Whistlestop High School. From there it snaked down some side streets before ending on the school's football field. The weather was cool and clear, ideal running weather. Fifteen minutes later the serious runners were crossing the finish line to the cheers from the bleachers.

In the middle of the pack Andy Parta ran beside his father, enjoying his company more than maximizing his speed. As they passed the midpoint he was happy to see Sam helping Sara and Kim pass out water. Their loud encouraging cheers gave the Partas a speed boost.

Likewise Gary Johnson partnered with Conner giving him tips on racing in a wheelchair as they traveled the course. The two crossed the finish line together.

At 9:30 the last of the runners crossed the finish line. The marching band which had been entertaining the crowd, took to the field. In perfect formation they performed the two pieces from last summer's parades. Then everyone stood at attention while they played the Star Spangled Banner.

After a brief thank you and infomercial from the American Diabetes Association, everyone was reminded that the annual town auction was the next weekend. The Kimsara crew quickly circulated passing out auction flyers. Finally the winners were announced. Most of the winning runners were from out of town. Many locals came in second or third in the various categories. The exception was in the ten to thirteen age group. Mary Smith came in first and was boisterously acknowledged. The only tie was in the wheelchair division.

After the ceremony many from the Kimsara group gathered to congratulate Conner. He introduced them to Gary Johnson.

RT acknowledged, "I saw you race last year. You were really fast. Why were you so slow today?"

"I do a lot of races. Winning is only one aspect of racing. Today I had the privilege of mentoring Conner through his first wheelchair race. That was more fun than winning. However, next time we meet in a race, Conner, I expect to be challenged by you." He laughed as he said it.

"I learned so much today. Thanks. However, I'll need a few years of practicing what you taught me before I'll be able to keep up with you. Thanks for all the tips."

"I never thought I would be racing against the wheelchair I donated to the American Legion. It's still in good racing form."

Conner's parents joined the group adding their thanks as the group dispersed.

Sara and Kim joined their parents directing the last of the traffic. RT helped his father pack up the timing equipment. Mary Smith celebrated by having dinner with her two mothers. All felt the run had been a success. Two weeks later the group would have a check for $2500, their share of the profits, to give to the Michels.

By that time The Kimsara Detective Agency would also receive official recognition as a non-profit organization thanks to the work of Sara and Andy's fathers.

Chapter 63

That Monday at school Sara congratulated Mary Smith.

"That wasn't the best part of my weekend. I found out that my aunt is my real mother and I'm not really adopted," gushed Mary.

Sara changed the subject as she remembered, "Wasn't your trailer destroyed in the tornado?"

"That was my aunt's trailer."

"The one who is really your mother, your birthmother?" Sara could relate to the confusion of having two mothers.

"Right, Sara."

"Sorry."

"It's okay. I was staying with her at the trailer the night of the tornado. Her boyfriend came over and told us to go to his house since it was safer. He moved out a lot of her stuff before the tornado struck. She has been debating on marrying him and moving into his house. Now she says the decision is easier to make. So it all works out."

The bell announcing the start of the school day scattered them to their respective homerooms.

At lunch Conner was again congratulated and then the group moved on to the upcoming auction. Emma reminded everyone, "If you're donating something to the auction, the committee needs it by Friday. You can drop it off at the Chamber of Commerce Office or if it is valuable, at the Whistlestop Credit Union."

Sara had already moved her necklace and a few other pieces of jewelry out of the family's lock box to the auction's box.

Abdi added, "We need to keep reminding everyone about the auction."

"We can't have too much advertisement. Everyone with a Facebook page should post a reminder this Friday," suggested RT.

"Peter, I think it's great that your father is broadcasting the auction at your restaurant for those who don't want to go to the auditorium," lauded Kim.

"He's only able to do it because Adam got the local cable station to cover it. Anyone with cable can watch it," noted Peter.

"But those who go to the restaurant will be contributing to our fundraising because your father is contributing a percentage of his profit from during the auction. Right, Peter?" Sara checked.

"Right. Dad sure appreciated that his restaurant's contribution was included on the flyers. Some customers wanted to contribute to the cause but can't be there on Saturday. He put out a donation jar at their request."

On Thursday, Emma shared, "My cousin said that the auctioneer expects a huge crowd based on the inquiries she's gotten. The auditorium may be too small. If that happens the overflow will go to the cafeteria and both will be linked through the schools' TV system."

"Do you usually have such a large crowd?" Sara asked.

"No, we're usually lucky to fill a third of the auditorium," admitted Emma.

"But the auction was never as heavily advertised," reminded Kim.

Chapter 64

On the day of the auction, a record crowd filled both the auditorium and cafeteria. About half were residents of Whistlestop. Based on the drivers licenses used to secure bidding numbers the rest were from all over the state with a few from Wisconsin.

The Whistlestop police circulated through the gathering crowd. As the crowd grew some Sherburne County police arrived, responding to Sheriff Nixon's's request. Two groups in tailored suits, dark glasses and briefcases walked into the auditorium from opposite doors. The ones in pinstripes sat on the home side of the auditorium. The gray suits settled on the visitors side. The sheriff felt their animosity electrifying the room. He called for more backup. When the state troopers arrived they confirmed that the suited groups represented two rival factions of the Minnesota Mafia. Their chauffeurs' drivers licenses secured their auction numbers. So the exact identities were unknown.

Having arrived early, Sara, Kim and Emma perched in the bleachers near their families. "Where did all these people come from?" Kim asked of no one in particular.

RT ambled by with a shocking answer. "The mafia is here."

"You mean they came all the way from Chicago for our auction?" Kim scoffed.

"No, Silly, the Minnesota Mafia," clarified RT as he settled near them.

"That's just an urban legend," corrected Sara's dad.

"No, sir. As we walked by the state troopers, they told the sheriff that in fact members of the mafia were present," RT declared authoritatively.

"Are we in danger?" whimpered Emma.

"I doubt it with all the police presence," assured RT. "I wonder what they will be bidding on."

Emma's cousin introduced the auctioneer who started with some antique furniture. Occasionally a bid came from one of the suited groups. They never stayed in the bidding long enough to actually buy the item until a modern painting came up for bid. Vibrant reds and yellows screamed from the canvas. Several people bid on it. At a thousand dollars only two bidders remained, the pinstripes and gray suits. They volleyed the price up to six thousand dollars before the pinstripes dropped out.

Emma commented, "My cousin doubted the painting would even bring in a hundred dollars. I wonder why it was so special to those two guys."

"Maybe they just didn't want the others to get it. That happens at auctions," Sara's dad proposed.

By the time the last category, jewelry, came up many had left, but not the mafia or any police. Each piece went for a couple of hundred dollars with occasional bids and purchases by the mafia. When the auctioneer held up Sara's necklace before she could start the bidding one of the pinstripes called out, "a thousand dollars."

The auctioneer's, "Do I hear a thousand fifty?" was countered with "two thousand."

The two factions fired counter bids at each other until the gavel dropped. Everyone gasped. As those accompanying the winning bidder rose, some police provided escort to the payment table. The rest fanned around the other group which exited without incident.

The police wondered among themselves what was so special about that necklace. One suggested mafia involvement. Several expressed disbelief that the mafia even existed.

"Weren't the mafia connected to prohibition?" Officer Jack Lewis pressed. "I thought they went out of business when drinking became legal."

"They shifted their business to gambling and other aspects of racketeering. They've kept a pretty low profile lately," the sheriff explained.

"Weren't they replaced by gangs?" Lewis proposed.

"Some gangs might have mafia ties. The mafia's bootlegging money, if invested well should be providing a comfortable living for the families. I wish I knew why they were here and what was so special about that necklace," pondered the sheriff as they walked out of the auditorium. He remembered a past conversation with Art Chaffins which he had dismissed earlier.

Chapter 65

Andy watched the auction from home with his mom and dad. He commented, "Those guys bidding on that painting look like criminals."

"I agree. They could have stepped right out of *The Godfather* movie," added his mother. "Joe, there isn't a real mafia nowadays, is there?"

"The Minnesota mafia families do exist. They became quite wealthy during prohibition. Until Hubert Humphrey's time, they ran Minneapolis. Lately they have been very low key, but I doubt if they've all died out."

"Gangs are more often mentioned," Ginger observed.

Andy redirected their attention to the TV. "That's Sara's necklace. She found it in a bag after her father died. It's worth $50,000. That would be a big help for Sam and his mom."

"Oh, my," his mother exclaimed as the bid went beyond $50,000. When the bidding ended they looked at each other in stunned silence.

Andy's phone rang. He answered, "Sam, would you believe it?"

"All that money..." stuttered Sam.

Andy interrupted, "You don't get it all, remember. You only get 80%."

"Andy, if we got ten percent we would be happy. Why did they bid so much?"

"How would I know?"

"I called to tell you my aunt plans to drop me off after dinner, if that's okay."

"Dad, Mom, is it okay if Sam comes back after dinner?"

"Fine, Son," his Father agreed.

"It's okay." Andy said. "See you then."

Before Andy could put his phone in his pocket, another call came.

"Sorry, I meant to call your father," the voice said.

"He's right here. Just a minute," Andy acknowledged while passing the phone to his father.

"Sorry, I dialed the wrong Parta. Got a minute?"

"Art, I'm glad you called. That auction was something else," Joe exclaimed.

"Something is the right word. Something's wrong with that obscene bid on Sara's necklace, Joe. The bidder paid with cashier's checks that kept the buyer anonymous. Who walks around with that much in cashier's checks?" Art gasped.

As Joseph Parta walked into his study and closed the door, he admitted, "The mafia, Art. I'm afraid what we feared is true."

"What can we do to protect Sara?" worried Art.

"Work with the FBI?" he hesitantly suggested. "Do you still have Kelly's contact information?"

"Yes."

"Have you shared it with the sheriff?"

"I did after Sara was shot but never heard any follow up. I think he did take it seriously with all the backup police at the auction. We've never had more than the Whistlestop police at past auctions. Come to think of it, I think FBI Agent Kelly was there."

"Does Sara know?"

"If she does, she didn't hear it from me. I'd rather she didn't know," Art sighed.

"Is that fair?"

"Is life fair?" Art sighed before hanging up.

Chapter 66

The next morning Art met Sara as they both descended the stairs. Sara admitted, "During the auction I felt like people were looking at me."

"Even though those who donated the auction items were never mentioned, many people knew that was your necklace," suggested her dad.

"But even before the necklace came up, from the very beginning, I felt people were watching me. Especially a bald guy in a suit on the other side of the auditorium. He looked familiar but I couldn't remember why. I took his picture." Sara found the picture on her phone and showed it to her parents.

Her dad recognized him immediately as FBI Agent JD Kelly. Not knowing what he should disclose he suggested, "Send that photo to my phone and I'll see if I can get him identified."

"Thanks, Dad," Sara exclaimed with guarded relief in her voice. "I can't believe auctioning my necklace means so much money for Sam and his mom. It was only worth $50,000."

Sara went to let the dogs back in. She made them wipe their dirty paws on the rags by the door.

Her mother opened the Sunday paper. Sara's necklace glared from the front page. The caption shrieked, "Mafia Property Returned." Art's heart sunk as he saw it. Quickly skimming it, he felt a little relief as he shared it with his wife.

"At least Sara isn't mentioned," Patty consoled.

"How do we tell her?"

"Tell who, what?" Sara asked as she walked into the kitchen and glanced at the spread newspaper. "Why is my necklace in the paper?" Seeing her parents stunned silence she added, "Mafia? Oh, that bald guy at the auction, I remember. He's an FBI agent who worked with? or was a friend of my father."

"JD Kelly?" suggested her dad.

Thoughtfully Sara tried remembering. "That name sounds right."

"The newspaper says that the necklace belonged to one of the mafia families." Patty continued reading, "While it couldn't be confirmed, sources say two factions of the family wanted to reclaim it. The vying parties' determination led to the largest sale in the history of Whistlestop's charity auctions."

"Notice that Sheriff Nixon refused to confirm the mafia connection," Art pointed out. "He explained the extra police were due to the size of the crowd, not who was in the crowd."

"How did my father get ahold of a piece of mafia jewelry?" questioned Sara. "Why did the paper I found with the necklace say it was made for me? What's the connection to the mafia?"

"That's a lot of questions. We may never get some of them answered." Then Patty remembered, "Somehow the mafia came up in a family discussion. Your father said something about being glad the family had no connection to it, if it really existed."

"His mother collected jewelry. She probably bought it from someone who needed the money. She wouldn't have worried if it had been stolen or not. She helped people, anyone who needed help. That's how she was," Art reported.

"I think it would be best if, Sara, you don't get named as the donor of the necklace," Patty suggested.

"I agree. I never was comfortable with it. Too bad so many at school know I donated it," Sara sighed.

Chapter 67

Sara and Kim discussed ways of disconnecting from the necklace. They texted the Kimsara regulars for ideas. As a result, Monday at lunch, Abdi handed Sara the following:

※

I received the necklace anonymously so I don't know its origin. I'm not sure why I received it. I tried to get permission to donate it but the giver seems to have vanished.

※

Sara read it out loud.

Abdi added, "If people ask if you got it from a man or woman, you don't know."

"You could counter with, 'What difference does it make if I got it from a plastic bag or crackerjack box? I still don't know exactly where it came from,'" suggested RT.

When Emma joined the group, she exclaimed, "Sara, your necklace, wow! Thanks for donating it."

"Emma, I'd like to detach my name from the necklace. The way I got it was strange. I'm not exactly sure who it came from. With the paper connecting it to the mafia I really don't want my name attached to it," pleaded Sara.

"I'll text that to my cousin." After finishing the text she admitted, "My cousin, Heather, hasn't done any of the auction followup yet. She said she'd have the final results on Tuesday or Wednesday after all the checks clear the bank."

"I figure with what we had donated to the auction Sam's mom should be getting quite a bit of money," Abdi calculated.

"Don't forget the $2500 from the race," Conner added. Some of the winners had donated their prize money back to the Diabetes Association.

"The $700 dollars from donations through our restaurant seems so small compared to that," Peter murmured.

"Every little bit helps," countered Andy as he and Sam joined the Kimsara group for lunch.

"My mom couldn't believe how much money you raised. She is afraid some of the checks will bounce so she won't believe it until she has the money safely in our bank account. Thanks, everyone for helping us," lauded Sam. "I don't know how we can repay you."

"No repayment is expected. We were just happy we could help," Sara acknowledged.

"Your necklace brought in a lot of money," complimented Sam.

"About that, I really don't want people to connect the necklace to me. I'm not sure why it was given to me. The paper said it got such a high bid because two mafia families were bidding on it," explained Sara. "Would you want to be connected with the mafia?"

"Guess not," Sam replied.

Everyone ate in silence for a few minutes. Some wondered why Andy had joined them but weren't sure how to find out.

Finally Andy explained, "I don't know how your Kimsara Detective Agency works but I would like your help on something else."

"What?" asked Kim.

"I think Mary Smith is in some kind of trouble," Andy said.

"Why?"

"That's part of the problem, Sara. I don't know what the problem is. I've seen her with some of the bullies in school. Twice she walked away from Herman, Tony and Jack crying. I don't really know her and didn't know what to do. So that's why we're here."

Sara admitted, "I know Mary. I'll see if she'll tell me."

Chapter 68

That afternoon Sara exited school to wait for her brother's girlfriend, Peaches. She saw Mary Smith on a bench, deep in thought and joined her.

"Hi, Mary," she greeted.

Mary looked worried and waited before answering, "Hi, Sara. I've been thinking about talking with you."

"About what?"

"Oh, things."

"What kind of things?"

"There's my mom, got to go," Mary said while gathering her things.

Sara reached in her backpack and pulled out her Kimsara Detective Agency card. "Call me sometime. I'd like to talk with you. You are the only one I know who, like me, has two moms."

Mary looked at the card, promising as she hurried to the car, "I will."

Sara spied Peach's bright yellow VW Beetle approaching. She considered her a dear friend. She had met her while in a coma after the accident that killed her family. Peaches visited her in the hospital with her new brother, Jerry, almost every day. When she returned to school, Peaches accompanied her, studying her recovery from the coma. Today they were celebrating the completion of that study.

"Peaches, your car always makes me smile," Sara greeted as she slipped in and buckled her seatbelt.

"That's why I bought it. Its happy personality serves me well." Peaches pulled away from the school. "Where do you want to go for dinner?"

"Anywhere, no preference."

After driving for a few miles, Peaches asked, "Have you been to the Pink Parfait?"

"Never hear of it."

"It just opened."

"Where?"

"On Hwy 10 toward St. Cloud. Up for trying it?"

"Sure. The name makes it sound like an ice cream shop."

"Let's see if the name fits," Peaches suggested as they parked in its nearly empty parking lot.

After entering Sara observed, "Not a lot of customers."

"I expected the inside to gush pink, not black and silver," commented Peaches. The hostess ushered them to a table and handed them silver and black menus.

"It's not girlie like the name suggests," Peaches noted.

"Good thing since most of the customers are men," Sara countered.

"That's unusual. So is the menu. One page has meals a lumberjack would order. The next one has salads."

Sara continued the analysis. "Then there's the burger page, followed by crepes. I don't see a parfait page."

"No desserts are listed. Maybe that's a separate menu," Peaches suggested. "Have you decided what you want to order?"

"The chicken crepe with asparagus and mushroom looks interesting. So does the shrimp and crab crepe."

"Why don't we get both and then share them?" Peaches offered as a server approached their table.

While waiting for the meal, Peaches displayed a looseleaf binder on the table. The title, *Recovering from a Coma: One Case*, was familiar. Sara examined the text for the first time. She scanned through the pages noticing different type peppering the pages.

"I planned on showing it to you before I submitted it, but ran out of time. Notice anything I got from you or your family are in this type." She pointed to a section in comic sans type. She continued pointing while explaining, "I used a Times font for research from books and lectures, like this section. My conclusions are in that italic type."

Sara honed in on the comic sans sections, noting, "You got me right."

"And your family?"

"I don't know what they were thinking. So far no surprises. Could I borrow this to read more of it?"

"That's your copy, Sara, do with it what you like. Check out page 77."

She turned to the page and read, "Recovered physically. The scars from the traumatic loss of her family should diminish over time though they will follow her all her life."

"All my life?" Sara moaned.

"Losing your family will always be part of your life. Has the pain lessened since it happened?"

"I guess so. The flashbacks have decreased and don't effect me as much."

Chapter 69

Their server appeared with their meals on pink striped plates. After dividing the entrees, both savored the crepes.

"Tasty. I'm not sure what spices were used. They sure are the right ones," relished Peaches.

"I'm glad we're having both. The tastes are so different. I don't know which one I like better."

"Paige, you made it," made them turn their heads toward an approaching petit chef in a pink jacket, pin striped black slacks and a black pillbox chef's cap over flaming red hair.

"Jackie, I wouldn't miss checking your place out." Gesturing she said, "This is my friend, Sara Cowley. Sara, this is my former roommate, Jackie Choux. She dropped out of college to become a chef."

"May I join you two for a few minutes?" Jackie perched on a chair before either could respond.

"Why did you name your restaurant, "Pink Parfait?" quizzed Sara.

"Good question. Wish I had a good answer. I like cooking French food but didn't think the St. Cloud area would welcome a French restaurant. When I gathered some of my culinary classmates for a brainstorming session we made a list of almost a hundred possible names. "Pink Parfait" stood out. No good reason. I liked the sound. A sale on a shipment of pink trimmed dinnerware confirmed my choice. I put together some French dishes like your crepes and some standard food for my first menu."

"I didn't see any parfaits on the menu," noted Sara.

"You have a dessert menu, right?" proposed Peaches.

"Not yet." Seeing her two patrons' confusion the chef added, "Right now at the end of the meal a dessert chef will come to your table with a cart of desserts. Each day it's different."

"Are they all parfaits?" inquired Sara.

"No, many are. Two students from the culinary arts program at the Tech College create parfaits and other French desserts as part of their internship. When I know what people like, we might create a set dessert menu. Or, we'll keep dessert a daily surprise.

"How was your meal?"

"Great. We couldn't decide what to order so we ordered two different crepes and shared them. Have you considered offering a sample crepe plate?" suggested Peaches.

"An interesting idea. If I did it as a special it might work," the chef thought. "Thanks for the idea. I need to get back to the kitchen. Here come the desserts. Enjoy."

A tall man dressed like Jackie, except in a white jacket, wheeled a cart to the table as their server removed their dishes.

"Hi, I am Mickey tonight's pastry chef. What would you like for dessert? After he described all of them, Sara selected an eclair while Peaches claimed the last cherry/chocolate parfait. They savored their choices in silence.

As Sara wiped the last drop of whipped cream from her plate, she declared, "Great meal. Thanks, Peaches."

"You're welcome, Sara. Thank you for letting me use you for my study."

As their server went by, Peaches requested the bill.

"It's on the house."

Shock registered on Peaches' face. "I'll be right back, Sara. Please wait here."

She walked toward the kitchen door sternly telling the first server she passed, "I need to speak to the head chef please."

A few moments later Jackie came out. Resolutely Peaches admonished, "Jackie, please, I want to pay for our meal. You're just starting. I'm sure your income isn't covering your expenses."

"Paige remember when I left college? My grandmother had just died. She surprised me with an inheritance that can keep the restaurant afloat for many years even if I brought in no income. As a matter of fact my accountant said I should make a half a million dollars in charitable contributions this year."

The amount triggered a memory. "Jackie, did you offer to match the donations raised by the Kimsara Detective Agency for a homeless family?"

"What if I did?"

"Thank you." Pointing back at their table she added, "That's Sara of the detective agency. For some reason she feared the mafia was behind the donation. Could you tell her you were behind the donation? She would appreciate knowing it wasn't the mafia."

In answer, Jackie walked over to Sara. "Are you Sara from the Kimsara Detective Agency?"

"Yes, why?"

She sat down. "Paige said you were afraid the mafia had matched your fundraising. I am telling you this in confidence." Peaches joined them. "I was the one who matched the Kimsara's fund raising. Both of you need to keep that secret, understand?"

"Why did you do it?" asked Sara.

"My best friend lost her mobile home in the recent tornado. I invited her to dinner and offered to help her financially. She wouldn't take any help. Her niece, Mary Smith, came with her. She asked me to put up an auction flyer. She also showed me the editorials. That gave me the idea of indirectly helping Josie. I called my lawyer and he arranged it. So I helped my friend and made my accountant happy."

"You also allowed us to help Sam and his mother. Thank you!" declared Sara feeling grateful that the mafia didn't match the donations. She stood and hugged Jackie.

"Come back again," invited Jackie.

"Only if we can pay," Peaches insisted.

"Definitely, next time," Jackie agreed as she walked them to the door.

Chapter 70

That evening as Sara finished her homework, her phone rang.

"Sara, I think I'm in a lot of trouble but I don't think I can talk about it with anyone."

"Mary, have you told your mom, either of your moms?"

"No," muttered Mary.

"Why not?"

"Because they said they would make it worse."

"Who?"

"I can't say," moaned Mary.

"Mary, are you talking about Herman, Tony and Jack?"

"How did you know?"

"Someone said they thought those three were bullying you. Are they?"

"Sara, remember the sixth grade movie shorts from last year?"

"Sorry, I went to a different school last year."

"Oh, everyone in sixth grade made a two minute video. Tony asked me to be in his even though I was only a fifth grader. He said he was doing an anti-drug ad. He had me pose in the park drinking beer and smoking. Then he had me drinking a lemonade which got me sleepy. I don't remember what happened. I woke up alone in the park. My clothes were all messed up and I had some bruises.

"The next day Tony thanked me for being so hot, too hot to use in his video."

Sara prodded, "Did you tell anyone?"

"No, I was too embarrassed," confessed Mary. "He showed it to Herman and Jack. They keep threatening to put it on the internet if I don't give them money, or do their homework."

"Have you seen it?"

"No."

"What if they really don't have a video?" proposed Sara. "You need to tell one of your parents, Mary. You really do?"

"I know," she murmured.

"Mary, I don't know what you should do. Could I check with my dad for ideas? I won't give him your name. Maybe he can help, if you really can't talk to one of your parents."

"You won't give him my name. Promise?"

"I won't," promised Sara as they hung up.

Sara went downstairs as her mother came up bidding her a goodnight. Her dad sat in the kitchen reading the newspaper.

"Dad, I need some advice."

"About?"

"A friend in school is in trouble and is afraid to tell her parents."

"What kind of trouble?"

Sara explained the situation.

"Has she told her parents?"

"No, I'm the first one she told. But the boy has told two of his friends and the three of them are making her life miserable."

"Do you know why she told you?"

Sara thought for a minute. Then she suggested, "A while ago she wanted our detective agency to help her with a problem which she solved on her own." Then another idea surfaced. "Maybe she told me because I knew the names of the boys who were harassing her. Andy Parta told me he saw the three bullying her and didn't know how to stop them."

After a few minutes of thoughtful silence, her father took a notebook from the counter and began writing as he spoke. "Has she seen the compromising video?"

"No and I suggested maybe they don't have one."

"Were any of these boys part of the computer hacking crowd?"

"Yes," she cautiously admitted.

"Keep encouraging her to tell her parents. Here are some other suggestions. Would you be willing to help her do them?"

After reading them she agreed, "Definitely and maybe she'll agree to have others help. Thanks, Dad, great ideas."

Chapter 71

The next morning as Sara ate breakfast, she texted the Kimsara regulars plus Andy Parta and Mary Smith: "I think Mary Smith is being bullied. If you see Herman, Tony and Jack near her, go and talk to Mary so she is never alone with any of these guys."

In a text to only Mary she added, "Can you meet me by the principal's office before the first bell? I'll explain."

"I'll try," bounced back.

On the bus, Kim grumbled to Sara, "What are we supposed to do? I don't even know who Mary Smith is."

"We'll work it out at lunch with everyone," Sara sighed wondering if she had done the right thing. When she entered school, to her relief, she saw an angry Mary Smith pacing outside the principal's office.

She advanced toward her holding out the notes from her dad. When Mary brushed them aside, Sara sternly ordered, "Read them."

As Mary did, her face relaxed and she agreed, "This might work."

"No one in Kimsara knows why you are being bullied. They don't need to know why. They don't even need to know who you are. We'll all keep our eyes open for these three. If they as a group or individuals try to corner anyone we'll step in and make sure their victim is not alone. That's all we are planning to do. If you want to follow any of the other suggestions it's up to you. Are you okay with that?"

"Yes, thanks," Mary whispered as the bell sent them to their home rooms.

At lunch Andy joined the Kimsara regulars. As Abdi joined the group he blurted, "Who is Mary Smith? Does everyone know who she is but me?"

A few did. Most didn't.

Sara countered, "Does everyone know Tony Criscitell, Jack Becker, and Herman Montel?"

"Of course. They're the biggest bullies in the school," Kim acknowledged. Everyone agreed.

"I get it," Peter exclaimed. "If we make sure biggest bullies in school never corner anyone not only will we help Mary Smith we'll stop a lot of kids from being bullied."

"But what do we say?" worried Emma.

"Let's brainstorm on some possible things we could say to either the bullies or the person, especially if we don't know them," suggested Abdi.

Conner immediately read from his notebook:

୬

1. Introduce yourself and walk with them away from the bullies quietly asking them if they need help.

2. Tell them you thought you heard their teacher or the principal was looking for them.
3. Act as if you know them and tell them you found something or wanted to explain something as you lead them away."

∞

"As one who has been bullied, I've thought a lot about what I wished others would do."

"We can approach in pairs or groups since we all will be watching for them and they usually hang out together," Peter offered.

"Good ideas," complimented Sara." Our goal would be ..."

"Isolate the bullies. Don't let them isolate anyone," Kim finished.

"Should we tell the principal or encourage kids to report the bullying?" Peter prodded.

"That could make the bullying worse," advised Andy.

"For now let's just keep our eyes on the three and help anyone they corner," Sara proposed as the bell ended lunch.

Chapter 72

During the next week the Kimsara regulars circulated in groups of two or three always keeping the three bullies in sight. Mary Smith had unknown support on three occasions when one or more of the trio approached her. On Thursday after school Sara joined Mary as Herman and Tony advanced.

"Get lost, Cowley. We have some private business with her," Tony snarled while pointing to Mary.

Mary calmly turned to Sara reporting, "They have a video of me that they threaten to put on the internet."

"Have you seen it?" pressed Sara.

"No, I haven't," Mary stated. Then she demanded, "Tony, I'd like to see the video. Do you have it on your phone?"

"Of course not," Tony sputtered. "It's on my computer at home."

"Is that the same computer the police checked when they caught you hacking the grades?" Sara jabbed.

"What do you care?" sneered Herman.

"I would hate to have Tony hauled off to jail again, this time for pornography," needled Sara.

"For that video?" mocked Herman. "You can't see anything. She's holding a beer bottle most of the rest is hazy. You can't even recognize her."

"So you were threatening me with a video that doesn't even exist?" Mary gasped.

"I thought you couldn't use the internet for two years as your punishment for hacking," reminded Sara.

"One year," corrected Tony.

"So what business did you have with Mary?" Sara nudged.

"Get lost, both of you," snapped Herman as he and Tony stomped off into the boys' bathroom.

To Sara's horror Abdi waved before going into the same bathroom. Yelling erupted. As Matt Nathan, the janitor, went by she pointed to the bathroom shouting, "Help. They're beating him up."

The janitor entered bellowing, "Stop. All of you, march to the principal's office."

Three dishoveled boys lumbered out. Abdi winked and gave a thumbs up as he passed the two girls. Herman held a paper towel against his bloody nose.

They sauntered down the hall toward a darkened office. The janitor poked his head inside then motioned the boys in while turning on the lights. "Vice principal, glad your still here. Caught these boys fighting in the bathroom, making a real mess."

"Thanks, Matt, I'll take care of this." He turned to the boys demanding, "Explain!"

Tony pouted, "This guy has been stalking us all week. We've had enough. We asked him to stop. Then for no reason he punched Herman. We had to defend ourselves."

"Interesting tale," commented the vice principal. "Abdi, why have you been hanging around Herman and Tony."

Abdi hesitated searching for the best words while looking from the vice principal to the others. "I heard they were starting up a lacrosse team and wanted to see if I could join, but I kept chickening out," he lied.

"Did you punch Herman?"

"Yes, sir," Abdi admitted.

"First?"

"Vice principal, I don't remember who struck first. The floor was wet and I kind of stumbled into them."

"You two boys, you are on probation. The terms require you to stay out of trouble in school. You need to find creative **positive** activities. Lacrosse would work."

Abdi immediately acknowledged, "They said they couldn't get enough interest in lacrosse after checking with everyone. I disagreed and we got a little carried away. Sorry, Sir."

Needing to get home the vice principal dismissed them with, "Get out of my office. I don't want a repeat of this."

As Abdi left the office, Sara and Mary joined him. Herman sniveled in Abdi's face, "What was that about?"

Abdi stepped back, challenging, "Did you want to get in trouble?"

Sara added, "Can you afford to get in trouble?"

Tony demanded, "You goody-goodies leave us alone."

"Not possible," Abdi vowed. "As long as you two, Jack, and your other pals are bullying kids we'll be watching you."

"And stopping you," threatened Sara.

"You can't. That's not fair," babbled Tony.

"Life's not fair," countered Sara.

The janitor approached asking, "Is there a problem here?"

"No, sir," Tony replied. "We're heading home."

As the two groups separated, Herman quietly warned, "Watch your backs."

"No, we won't," Abdi yelled a little too loud. The janitor looked back at the group.

"Everything's okay," Sara noted while waving to the janitor.

Abdi continued in a quieter voice, "Don't threaten us. As long as you are bullying kids in this school you need to watch **your** back. We're eradicating bullies. If you don't want us following you, you need to change. We aren't."

He turned and joined Mary and Sara leaving school while the others turned toward the gym.

Chapter 73

On Friday the Kimsara regulars gathered at their usual table. Conner for once arrived first and spoke. "Thanks, everybody. This has been a great week."

"What do you mean?" Kim countered.

"No one spilled anything on me, knocked into my wheelchair, pushed my notebook to the floor or made rude comments," boasted Conner. "The funny thing is every time I saw one of the usual suspects approach, two kids appeared. Some I did not know. This anti-bullying campaign is great. How did everyone get on board?"

"Facebook, Twitter, Snapchat, Instagram, you name it," Emma confirmed.

"Who started the Whistletops Bullies Website?" puzzled Sara.

When everyone denied doing it Abdi suggested, "I'll bet it's RT."

"What did I do?" RT questioned as he sat down.

"RT, did you set up the Whistletops Bullies Website?" pressed Kim.

"No. I must say whoever did is very clever."

"I agree. Everyone in school knows who Mack Wrecker, Skyler Penny, Sherman Letnom, Bonie Talker and the rest really are," Abdi smirked. "Some of the others were a surprise to me. I never would have considered them bullies."

"When Emma told me about the website listing the school bullies, I figured it would be closed down quickly for defamation of character. When I saw the name changes, even changing the town's name, I had to give the website builder credit for the genius idea," admired RT.

"I like how a lot of the incidents happened at away games with the team from Lake Wobegon," observed Sara.

"Where is Lake Wobegon anyway?" probed Kim.

"No where. It's a made up town," Sara explained.

Abdi's cousin, Isad Ahmed stopped by their table. "Congratulations on your fund raising." Kimsara had helped her awhile ago when someone stole her laptop.

The group began squeezing together to make room for her. She motioned for them to stop and joined her friends at another table.

After a few minutes of eating in silence, Kim asked, "Should we keep following the bullies?"

"I don't think we need to since everyone in school is watching them," Abdi recommended.

All agreed.

When Sara left the table she almost knocked into Andy Parta. "Sorry, Andy, I wasn't watching where I was going," apologized Sara.

"Neither was I," Andy confessed.

"Saturday, Sam and his mom will get their money from the auction," Sara beamed.

"I can't believe you guys raised so much for them," Andy muttered in a very flat voice.

"Andy, are you okay?"

"Yeah, it's been harder coming back to school than I expected. I'm not the same person. My old friends want the old Andy back."

"Do you?"

"Sara, sometimes I think I do. I feel responsible for Sam and they don't want me hanging around him."

"Has Sam made any friends in school?"

"He has and I would rather hang around with them. But Tony keeps on insisting that we get together and expanded our science project from last year. I would rather do one with Sam. But I don't know if he will go to our school next year. It all depends on where they end up living."

"What was your project?"

"The Amazing Cockroach," Andy announced sweeping his arms out in mock grandeur.

"Really?" After a thoughtful pause, Sara added, "That does fit him."

"And the old Andy, not me."

"Well, just tell him you don't want to do it."

"Do you know how hard it is to say no to Tony?"

"Andy, we need to stop these bullies. You have to stand up to him," insisted Sara.

Before Andy could object, they had walked into English class and separated. Both had the problem on their mind and jotted down notes throughout the class. At the end of the class each handed the other a torn notebook page.

Andy read:

~

Don't do it alone.
Have a science project with Sam already approved.
If Sam won't be here next year, someone else could take his place.
You can stand up to Tony.

~

Sara read:

~

Get project on diabetes approved for Sam and me.
Have others around when I tell Tony
Tell him I don't like cockroaches.
I can do it.

~

After reading the notes they exchanged smiles as they headed to different classes.

Chapter 74

That evening Andy and Sam explored the internet for a possible science project that related to diabetes. "Most of these are just giving information," noted Andy. "I'd like to do something that involves real science experimenting."

"Me to," agreed Sam. "Sugar is not a healthy food. But sometimes my mom needs to eat candy or she can go into a coma."

"She has to watch how much sweet stuff she eats, right?" Andy pondered.

"Sweets and something called carbs. She also has to take insulin because her body can't handle sugar like ours can."

"Here's one on how insulin works," suggested Andy. "But it doesn't give us ideas on experiments."

Sam pointed to a listing farther down. "How about 'How to measure the sugar in your food?' We could measure a lot of different foods."

Andy's eyes lit up as he shared, "What if we measured the sugar in the foods served in the cafeteria?"

"That would be easier in our other school, but here we have so many choices. That would be a lot of foods."

"We've got lots of time. We could do the most popular foods or the ones we think would be the healthiest. Our project could be, "Is cafeteria food safe for a diabetic to eat?"

"That sounds good. What do we do next?"

"We need to get it approved by Mr. Olson, the science fair director. We could email him our topic and an outline."

Before the boys went to bed they had emailed Mr. Olson:

Science project proposal

Is cafeteria food safe for a diabetic to eat?
Why diabetics need to watch how much sugar they eat?
How to measure the sugar in foods?
Sugar content of some cafeteria foods.

Andy Parta and Sam Michel

The next morning as they were getting ready for school they found an email approving their project. Andy printed it out and tucked it in his pocket.

At lunch Sam and Andy set their lunches down on an empty table. Immediately Tony, Jack and Herman joined them.

Tony began, "Andy, we need to get our science project okayed." He turned and addressed Kim, Sara and Abdi who had joined the group. "We're discussing science projects. Go find another table."

Ignoring him, Sara asked, "Andy and Sam what did you decide to do yours on?"

"Cockroaches," interrupted Tony. "Andy and I are polishing up last year's project."

"No, Tony," Andy stated. "Sam, tell everyone about our project."

As Andy rifled through his pockets, Sam explained, "We're going to see if our cafeteria food is safe for a person with diabetes to eat."

"Lame idea," disparaged Tony. "You'll never get it approved."

"Already got approval," Andy declared as he passed around the email.

Isad Ahmed sat nearby composing an entry for her Whistletops website about a fictional science fair with projects on cockroaches, killer spiders and rotting food.

Chapter 75

The first Saturday in May the Kimsara crew gathered at city hall for the distribution of the Whistlestop Charity Auction funds. Sam, his mother and aunt entered with the Partas.

Heather Wilcox approached the microphone. "Thank you for coming. Whistlestop outdid its usual generosity. Thanks to all who donated and bought items at the auction, we can give The United Way this check for $482, 067.85."

Approaching Heather, Natalie McCormick beamed. She took the check and announced, "We have exceeded our fundraising goal and will be able to continue supporting existing programs, help the victims of the recent tornado and meet new needs as they arise."

Everyone clapped as she returned the mike to Heather and sat down.

Heather announced, "We are able to present a check to the Michels because the Kimsara Detective Agency got involved. This landmark amount was possible because an anonymous donor matched the funds raised after editorials suggested boycotting their fund raisers because local causes were more important. We are grateful to that donor whoever you are." She paused as everyone clapped.

When it quieted, she continued, "I invite the Michels to come up."

Ava walked from the back. She wore a simple olive green pants suit. Sam walked beside her.

Ginger Parta sat a little straighter recognizing the outfit she had donated to the Salvation Army. She felt so connected to the world around her. She surprised Andy with a sideways hug. He smiled and squeezed her hand.

Heather began speaking, "For those who do not know, I would like to introduce Ava and Sam Michel."

The crowd clapped while Ava blushed. As the room settled, Heather continued, "We are so pleased to present the Michels with a check for $321,622.19." Again the crowd applauded.

Ava took the check and mike. She tried several times to speak above the noise, finally she succeeded. "Thank you. The generosity of the Whistlestop community is overwhelming. Who would expect students from here to be concerned about one homeless family in Wisconsin? I didn't, but your concern allows me to pay off all my outstanding medical bills and make a downpayment on a home in this community." Between her tears of gratitude, she finished with, "Most important, it allows me to provide a home for my son, Sam. Thank you."

Everyone was on their feet applauding.

As the group broke up a few reporters mingled. One approached Sara asking, "Where did Kimsara get that mafia necklace?"

Sara gave her rehearsed answer. "We are not sure exactly who it came from. It appeared after my family died in an accident. So it's origin will always be a mystery."

"Did you expect it to go for $400,000?"

"No," Sara admitted as she turned to join her family congratulating the Michels.

www.ingramcontent.com/pod-product-compliance
Lightning Source LLC
Chambersburg PA
CBHW071452040426
42444CB00008B/1303